Documents and Debates

The Unification of Italy
Second edition

Michael Morrogh

09/03

FLL 02/16816

945·08 MOR

First edition 1991
Second edition 2002
Published by
PALGRAVE MACMILLAN
Houndmills, Basingstoke, Hampshire RG21 6XS and
175 Fifth Avenue, New York, N.Y. 10010
Companies and representatives throughout the world

PALGRAVE MACMILLAN is the global academic imprint of the Palgrave Macmillan division of St. Martin's Press, LLC and of Palgrave Macmillan Ltd. Macmillan® is a registered trademark in the United States, United Kingdom and other countries. Palgrave is a registered trademark in the European Union and other countries.

ISBN 1–4039–0066–3

This book is printed on paper suitable for recycling and made from fully managed and sustained forest sources.

A catalogue record for this book is available from the British Library.

A catalogue record for this book is available from the Library of Congress

10 9 8 7 6 5 4 3 2 1
11 10 09 08 07 06 05 04 03 02

Printed and bound in Great Britain by J.W. Arrowsmith, Bristol

Contents

Using this Book

The author's introduction puts the period as a whole into perspective, highlighting the central issues, main controversies, available source material and recent developments. Each section carries its own brief introduction, which sets the documents into context. A wide variety of source material has been used in order to give the pupils the maximum amount of experience. The questions vary in difficulty, but aim throughout to compel the reader to think in depth by the use of unfamiliar material. Historical knowledge and understanding will be tested, as well as basic comprehension. Students are encouraged by the questions to assess the reliability of evidence, to recognise bias and emotional prejudice, to reconcile conflicting accounts and to extract the essential from the irrelevant. Some questions, *marked with a star*, require knowledge outside the immediate extract and are intended for further research or discussion based on the student's general knowledge of the period.

Acknowledgements

The author and publisher wish to thank the following for permission to use copyright material:

Oxford University Press for extracts from *The Political Life and Letters of Cavour* by A. J. Whyte, 1930; Peters Fraser and Dunlop Group Ltd, on behalf of the author, for extracts from *Daniele Manin and the Venetian Revolution of 1848–9* by Paul Ginsborg, Cambridge University Press, 1979; Yale University Press for extracts from *These Sad but Glorious Days*, edited by L. J. Reynolds and S. B. Smith (1991), copyright © L. J. Reynolds and S. B. Smith 1991.

Every effort has been made to trace all the copyright holders, but if any have been inadvertently overlooked the publisher will be pleased to make the necessary arrangement at the first opportunity.

Italy before 1859

Introduction

How can the *Risorgimento* not be an heroic theme? Here we have the 'resurgence' or national revival of a nation considered by many to be the epicentre of civilisation, twice the leader of Europe (materially under the Romans, then culturally in the Renaissance), yet until the mid-nineteenth century divided into separate states and languishing under foreign rule or dilapidated autocrats. Then comes an explosion of popular nationalism, unsuccessful in 1848/9, but ten years later uniting almost all the peninsula into one country. Few other historical episodes can match the grand sweep and suddenness of this movement.

The dramatis personae would seem to be equally satisfying. Among the heroes are a team of strong individuals, each playing a complementary part in the struggle: Cavour, mastermind of the entire operation in Turin and genius at the diplomatic game; Garibaldi, the photogenic and outrageously successful guerrilla leader; Mazzini, the visionary poet whose words enlisted thousands; bluff King Victor Emmanuel, who ensured Piedmont's stabilising role. In the wings were Napoleon III of France, whose troops were vital for military victory; and those benevolent English statesmen who watched over and encouraged the whole process.

The villains are here too: the imperial Austrians, subjugators of the Venetians and Milanese; the obscurantist Pius IX; down in Naples, the Bourbons, their very name a throwback to the *ancien régime*. Sometimes included in the demonology is Napoleon III again, this time wearing his reactionary hat as protector of the Papal States.

The above description is a deliberately broad caricature, but the point is that for a long time commentators did adopt the general line that the unification of Italy was the inevitable progression of a nation fighting as one on the road to independence. The leading figures might have disagreed on occasion, the ways and means were sometimes argued over, but essentially the *Risorgimento*, they claimed, was an harmonious, coherent movement.

The writings of the English historian Denis Mack Smith were among the first to crack this consensus. Essentially he exposed the rifts between the leaders, in particular Cavour and Garibaldi, with the former emerging a less than gleaming example of Italian nationalism. (Chapter 7 will detail their shifting relationship over Garibaldi's Sicilian expedition.) Historians now have to consider whether Italy was formed out of the conflict rather than co-operation between these heroes. Much of the venerable canvas has had to suffer extensive cleaning and reworking to the extent of becoming a new picture altogether.

Any collection of documents on this subject inevitably is going to concentrate on Cavour's correspondence, and the student has to handle these with caution. Cavour wrote with such verve, humour and fluency that he seems to take all readers, and not just recipients, into his confidence. The tendency to believe his remarks on account of his style is especially hard to resist when Cavour is being winningly frank and revealing.

Of course no document can be taken at its face value. A number of questions have to be asked in each case. Who is the addressee; what is his profession; where is he based? Are the communications private letters, official announcements, cabinet minutes, instructions to ambassadors, later reminiscences? It is surprising how often the same information changes meaning depending on its destination. One of the advantages of studying history through documents is to acquire an excellent nose for cant and special pleading. Although the participants in this field were not particularly deceitful by nature, the circumstances often dictated subterfuge and insincere opinions. It will be the reader's job to scrape away the protestations and discover the true intentions and worth of these extracts.

Besides letters and official business, there exist diaries and memoirs. Those for our period have a limited use. Garibaldi's memoirs, for example, were written long after these years and exhibit understandable bitterness at his treatment. Even diaries, ostensibly composed on the spot, can be less than reliable. With the knowledge that unification had succeeded, and that various policies and characters ridiculed at the time were now part of the glorious nationalist tapestry, the temptation to edit before publication was too hard to resist for some.

Foreign dispatches are usually reliable sources, because the writers tend to be observers rather than actors. The reports of the British representative at Rome are a good sample of relatively disinterested comment. But the diplomatic corps was human enough to harbour prejudice and had consequent axes to grind – the British consul at Venice in 1849, for example, or the French ambassador at Rome in 1860. French representatives indeed had an awkward time, pulled between the Foreign Ministry in Paris and the Emperor's frequently private diplomacy, and their correspondence sometimes betrays this desire to please different masters.

Among the extracts are two sections from an Italian novel, which has Sicily in 1860 as the background for some of its chapters. These 'documents' might make the purists blench, but they provide a sensibility denied to the historian. They could also serve to introduce some readers to a celebrated work.

The approach is largely chronological. While there are recognised terminal points to the *Risorgimento* (in our case 1861, though 1866, 1870 and 1918 completed territorial unification), there is no clear beginning to the business. It makes sense, however, to start by looking at Italy in 1815; then the stirrings of national opinion and the various theories of unification. Two chapters are devoted to the risings in 1848–9 and three to 1859–60. In between are chapters on Piedmont in the 1850s, as it recovered from the earlier episode and reformed itself to benefit from the latter. This arrangement of events might give one the impression that Piedmont (and Cavour) planned out the whole final stage. It is certainly possible to hold this view, and some documents will support it; but the alternative version – that opportunism reigned and prominent statesmen were as surprised as anyone at the outcome – is just as tenable.

I   Obstacles to Italian Unification

Introduction

Although the Treaty of Vienna largely restored the Italian states of the eighteenth century, the effect of the intervening years of French occupation could not be effaced. Napoleon had shown that Italian boundaries could be redrawn and even a 'kingdom of Italy' established (albeit covering just part of northern Italy). The later years of French rule also created a binding sense of Italian nationalism among those in opposition; a nationalism which easily transferred itself against the subsequent occupying power after 1815 – Austria.

If nationalist feeling can be traced back to the early nineteenth century (and even before), historians must then ask why Italy was not unified earlier than the 1860s. Partly it was because nationalism had to challenge local allegiance. Most Italians gave their loyalty to the city state or principality. Different dialects, customs, and innumerable trade barriers encouraged this particularism. That grand enemy to liberalism and nationalism, Prince Metternich, was perhaps not far off the mark with his famous phrase that 'Italy' was a geographical expression.

The minority who did look beyond their immediate frontier were unable to agree either on the form of unity or the method to achieve it. First into the field was a shadowy organisation called the Carbonari. Its programme was clear about expelling the Austrians and recalcitrant rulers, but vague on the nature of the new Italy – whether a monarchy or republic, a centralised state or confederation of separate states. One Carbonaro dissatisfied by such orderless planning was Giuseppe Mazzini, who formed his Young Italy movement with the precise intention of fomenting an uprising by Italians alone to make a unitary, democratic republic. This was strong meat for other nationalists, who preferred less extreme solutions, with some of the rulers and their institutions being retained in a loose federation.

All agreed, however, on the expulsion of the Austrians. Lombardy and Venice were part of their empire, and the

Austrians enjoyed indirect influence over most of the other states. Nothing could be done to unite Italy unless their power was broken. But the Carbonari attempts of 1820–1 and 1831–2, and subsequent Mazzinian-inspired risings all failed, crushed by Austrian troops, local rulers and sometimes the two in conjunction.

1 Italy after the Treaty of Vienna

(a) *A Piedmontese observes the political situation after 1815*

It remains to describe the situation in the country today. Sicily and the Kingdom of Naples have gained by becoming subject once more to a single [Bourbon] sovereign; their former relations and their commercial interests demanded this union.
5 Piedmont has recovered its old dynasty; it has a government of its own again and an army. Its annexation of Genoa, necessitated by recent political events, had long been required by nature, for Liguria had trade but not territory, whereas Piedmont had agricultural produce and no market for it. Their
10 reunion should henceforth be the source of greater prosperity for both countries, and greater security. But strong as this state is on the side which faces France, it is exposed where it confronts the Austrian possessions. Moreover, occupying as it does such a limited area, with only a small population and military
15 forces greatly disproportional to those of its neighbours, it cannot but live in continual anxiety.

Austria, possessing the richest and most fertile regions of the peninsula, besides nearly a quarter of the total Italian population, and also holding sway over Tuscany, Parma and Modena
20 through princes of her ruling House, cuts Italy in half and is its actual mistress. On the other hand, by the re-establishment of the entire temporal domain of the Pope, two and a half millions of Italians have been plunged afresh into a state of absolute nullity, and the King of Naples, relegated to the end
25 of the peninsula, has no longer any means of contributing to the defense of Italy; while on the other hand Austria threatens the King of Piedmont on his flank, pressing upon him with all her weight, and by merely calling up her garrisons in Lombardy could sweep down upon him, reach his capital in a
30 couple of marches and destroy his resources …

… there will always be blood to shed until Italy is left alone, with all foreigners alike excluded. Neither France nor Austria will ever consent to yield to the other. Neither of them will feel safe while the other has a foot in Italy. And so, half
35 through fear, half through cupidity, they will continue to disturb the tranquillity of Europe. Even if they agreed to share

Italy between them, they would still be in a constant state of suspicion, each of them thinking out a way of increasing her share or driving out her rival altogether. It is obvious, there-
40 fore, that so long as this rivalry subsists, Europe can hope for no real peace. The only means of extinguishing it would seem to be the establishment in the north of Italy of a state strong enough to defend the Alps and bar the gates of Italy to all for-eigners … Piedmont has nothing in common with the
45 Dauphine, nor Venetia with Austria; whereas each part of northern Italy is at exactly the same stage of civilisation; there is a general consensus of opinion and a community of interests; in fact, in many ways the inhabitants resemble one another far more than they do those of Tuscany, Rome and Naples.

> Memo by the Piedmontese ambassador to Tsar Alexander, March 1818, from D. Mack Smith, *The Making of Italy, 1796–1866* (London, 1988) pp. 25, 28–9.

(b) Stendhal learns the extent of Italian localism

50 I discovered signor Cavaletti alone in his box. 'Will you do me the favour,' he began, 'not to let your mind be seduced by the manifold denunciations against the Church, the Aristocracy and the Sovereign Princes of Italy, which you hear at every hand? Instead, enquire philosophically, and consider the six focal
55 centres of activity which control the destiny of the eighteen million inhabitants of Italy: Turin, Milan, Modena, Florence, Rome and Naples. You do not need telling that these different peoples are very far from forming a homogenous nation. … Each city detests its neighbours, and is mortally detested in
60 return. It follows therefore that our rulers have no difficulty in the fulfilment of their aim: *divide ut imperes*. …

Modena and Turin are as clay in the hands of the Jesuits. Piedmont is the most monarchical country in Europe. The ruling oligarchy in Austria has still not progressed a step beyond
65 the notions of a Joseph II, who for want of anything better, passes in Vienna for a great man; it constrains the priesthood to respect the laws and to abstain from intrigue; but in all other respects, it treats us as a colony.

Bologna, and indeed the whole of the Romagna, are a con-
70 stant nightmare to the Court of Rome; so Consalvi sends a Cardinal to govern the country, with orders to make himself beloved – and he obeys! Consalvi, who wields unchallenged authority as Minister in Rome, is an ignoramus blessed with mother-wit and a sense of moderation; and he is well aware
75 that, in Bologna, and indeed throughout the Romagna, the Italian people have preserved some traces of that ancient

energy inherited from the Middle Ages. In the Romagna, when a mayor proves too consummate a scoundrel, he is assassinated; and not a single witness will ever be brought to light to testify against the murderer. Such brutal behaviour in the Bolognese is abhorrent to their nearest neighbours, the citizens of Florence. The celebrated government of the Grand-Duke Leopold, successor to the appalling despotism of the Medici, has transformed the Florentines into a race of holy-minded *castrati*. All passion is extinct within their souls, save a love of handsome liveries and a taste for the prettiness of religious processions. Their Grand-Duke adores money and women, and behaves like a father to his children. At bottom, he is as indifferent towards them as they are towards him; but they need only cast a glance at what is happening in the world outside to view each other with rational affection ...

In Italy, the extreme outposts of civilisation follow the course of the Tiber. Southward of this river, you may discover all the energy and all the happiness of a race of savages. In the Papal State, the only law in force is that of the Catholic faith, which means the *performance of ritual*. Of its quality, you may judge by its effects. Under its authority, all moral philosophy is forbidden, as favouring a *spirit of individual enquiry*

The Kingdom of Naples is confined to this one city, which alone among all the towns of Italy has the tone and the bustle of a true capital.

Its government is an absurd monarchy in the style of Philip II, which yet manages to preserve a few rags and tatters of administrative discipline, a legacy from the French occupation. It is impossible to imagine any form of government of more abysmal insignificance, or with less influence to wield upon the populace ...

The Duke of Modena has refused to allow the stage-coach to cut across his estates, on the grounds that "all travellers are Jacobins" ...

> From Stendhal's journal, 1817, in D. Beales, *The Risorgimento and the Unification of Italy* (London, 1981) pp. 119–21.

(c) *Manzoni regrets the lack of a national language*

Show me in Italian literature that uniformity of language can go along with variety of style, and I will then agree that Italy is like other countries where this kind of problem does not exist. If you could show me such a uniformity, we could forgo what would then be the superfluous task of trying to create a common tongue.

Granted, too, that over all Italy there is a common spoken language of a kind. But suppose you have a group of

Milanese, not just ordinary people, but well-to-do and well educated; and suppose they are talking in the local dialect, as
120 would be the normal custom throughout Italy; then introduce into the circle a Piedmontese, a Bolognese, a Venetian, or a Neapolitan, and watch them give up dialect and try their hand at our common Italian language. Tell me if their conversation goes as before; tell me if those Milanese can
125 touch various subjects with the same richness and sureness of vocabulary. Will they not have to use a generic or imprecise term when before they had a precise one? ... Or in desperation perhaps they will use a word they know is not Italian, trying to dress it up to look as plausible as they can. ... Or
130 perhaps they will use some Italian suffix and otherwise try to Italianise a Milanese word or phrase, the very thing they would find ridiculous if others did it. ... And is this really to possess a language in common?

... Existing habits will not change except insofar as we can
135 find a common language which could serve the same purpose, a language which would alter our manner of speech but not lessen our powers of expression.

Alessandro Manzoni, 1836, in D. Mack Smith, *The Making of Italy, 1796–1866* (London, 1988) pp. 71–3.

Questions

a   In extract (a), why was the acquisition of Genoa so important for Piedmont?

b   Explain how Austria 'cuts Italy in half and is its actual mistress' (lines 20–1).

c   What projected state did the Piedmontese ambassador envisage; and what part was Russia expected to play?

d   How does extract (b) contradict extract (a) in terms of north Italian localism?

★ e   Who were the Jesuits? Explain extract (b)'s attitude to them.

f   Why did the Romagna develop a separate identity from the rest of the Papal States?

g   Account for the Duke of Modena's opinion of 'travellers'.

★ h   How did Manzoni personally encourage the development of a 'common language' which he called for in extract (c)?

i   How can these extracts be used to support the view that Italian unity was a chimera in the years immediately after 1815?

2 The growth of secret societies: the Carbonari and Young Italy

(a) *Instructions of the Carbonari*

Aim of the Order. The independence of Italy, our Country. To give her a single, constitutional government, or at least to unite the various Italian governments in a confederation; all governments, however, shall be based on a constitution, freedom of
5 the press and of worship, the same laws, currency and measures.

    Methods of the Order. To spread liberal ideas and communicate them to adherents, friends and clerics, by firmly convincing them of the unfortunate state of affairs in our Mother Country.
10 The press, gatherings and private conversations are opportune means. Cunning and perseverance are needed and, above all, the eradication of all kinds of prejudice. The unprejudiced peasant is more enthusiastic than the rich man, the property owner, and is therefore more useful.

    From the instructions of the 'Society of Guelph Knights', in S. J. Woolf, *The Italian Risorgimento* (London, 1969) p. 41.

(b) *Mazzini's views on the Carbonari*

15 Whispers were rife amongst us of a revival of carbonarism. I watched, questioned, and searched on every side, until at last a friend of mine – a certain Torre – confessed to me that he was a member of the sect, or, as it was called in those days, the Order, and offered me initiation. I accepted.
20   While studying the events of 1820 and 1821, I had learned much of carbonarism, and I did not much admire the complex symbolism, the hierarchical mysteries, nor the political faith – or rather the absence of all political faith – I discovered in that institution. But I was at that time unable to attempt to form
25 any association of my own; and in the carbonari I found a body of men in whom – however inferior they were to the idea they represented – thought and action, faith and works, were identical. Here were men who, defying alike excommunication and capital punishment, had the persistent energy ever
30 to persevere, and to weave a fresh web each time the old one was broken. And this was enough to induce me to join my name and my labours to theirs ...

    [Mazzini was betrayed and briefly imprisoned in 1830]

    Meanwhile, through the medium of my friends in Genoa,
35 I continued to exhaust every effort to strike a spark of true life from carbonarism ... I contrived to tell my friends to seek interviews with many carbonari of my acquaintance, all

of whom, however, proved to be terror-struck and repulsed both my friends and their proposals. ... The silly terror
40 shown by the carbonari in that important moment, my own long meditations on the logical consequences of the absence of all fixed belief or faith in that association ... all confirmed me in the conviction I had acquired some months before, that carbonarism was in fact dead, and that, instead of
45 wasting time and energy in the endeavour to galvanise a corpse, it would be better to address myself to the living, and seek to found a new edifice upon a new basis.

It was during these months of imprisonment that I conceived the plan of the association of Young Italy. I meditated
50 deeply upon the principles upon which to base the organisation of the party, the aim and purpose of its labours – which I intended should be publicly declared, the method of its formation, the individuals to be selected to aid me in its creation, and the possibility of linking its operations with those
55 of the existing revolutionary elements of Europe.

Guiseppe Mazzini in D. Mack Smith, *The Making of Italy, 1796–1866* (London, 1988) pp. 44, 46–7.

(c) *Mazzini's programme for Young Italy*

Young Italy is the brotherhood of Italians who believe in a law of *Progress* and *Duty* – are convinced that Italy is called to be a nation – that she can make herself one through her own strength – that the failure of past attempts is due not to
60 weakness, but to the poor leadership of the revolutionary parties – that the secret of strength lies in constancy and unified effort. Joined in association, they consecrate their thought and action to the great aim of making Italy once again a nation of free and equal men, *One Independent* and
65 *Sovereign* ...

Young Italy stands for the republic and unity. ... The *Republic*, because Italy really has no basis for a monarchy; ... because the Italian tradition is wholly republican, as are its greatest memories and the progress of the nation; because
70 monarchy was established when our decline began, and assured our downfall; because if monarchy was the aim of the Italian revolution, all the encumbrances of the monarchical system would inevitably be brought with it – concessions to foreign courts, respect for and faith in diplomacy, repression
75 of the masses who alone have the strength to save us, and authority vested in the king's men who gain by betraying us. This would unquestionably destroy the revolution ... *Unity*, because without unity there can be no true nation – because without unity there is no strength, and Italy, surrounded by

80 united, powerful and jealous nations, needs to be strong
    above all – because by destroying the unity of the great
    Italian family, Federalism would destroy at its roots the
    mission which Italy is destined to fulfil for humanity –
    because all the objections against the unitary system amount
85 to objections against a system of centralisation and adminis-
    trative despotism which has nothing to do with unity. ...
    The life of each community must be free and sacred.
    Administrative organisation must have a wide basis, and reli-
    giously respect the freedom of the communes; but political
90 *organisation*, destined to represent the Nation in Europe, must
    be one and central ...

    The means of fulfilling the aims of *Young Italy* are Education
    and Insurrection. These two methods must be made to work
    in agreement and harmony. Education, by writing, example
95 and word, must always preach the necessity of insurrection,
    and when it succeeds must provide a principle of national
    education ...

    Convinced that Italy can free herself by her own strength –
    that to found a Nation it is necessary to be conscious ... of
100 nationality, and that this consciousness cannot be obtained if
    insurrection is achieved or triumphs through foreign hands
    ... *Young Italy* is resolved to take advantage of foreign events,
    but not to allow the time and character of insurrection to
    depend on them.

    Mazzini, 1831, in S. J. Woolf, *The Italian Risorgimento*
    (London, 1969) pp. 48–9.

Questions

a In extract (a) explain what is meant by 'constitutional
   government' (line 2).
b In extract (b) why should the carbonari have to defy
   excommunication (line 28–9)?
c Are Mazzini's criticisms of the carbonari in extract (b)
   confirmed in any way by extract (a)?
d Compare the aims of the carbonari and Young Italy.
e Identify Mazzini's use of rhetoric in extract (c).
f How did Young Italy's proclaimed methods differ from
   the carbonari?

3 Theories of unification

(a) Papal confederation

Italy has within herself all the conditions of her national and political Risorgimento, without recurring to internal upheavals or to
foreign imitations and invasions. Italian union cannot be obtained
by revolutions. The principle of Italian union is the Pope, who
5 can unify the peninsula by means of a confederation of its princes.
Advantages of an Italian league. Federal government is connatural
to Italy and the most natural of all governments. Evils of excessive
centralisation. The security and prosperity of Italy cannot be
achieved otherwise than by an Italian alliance. Foreigners cannot
10 prevent this alliance, and, far from opposing it, they ought to
desire it. Excuse of the Author for entering upon discussion of
affairs of state. Opinion emerges from small beginnings, but must
be educated by the wisdom of the nation. Two provinces above
all ought to co-operate to foster the opinion which favours Italian
15 unity: Rome and Piedmont. Sympathy of Rome for peoples, and
its impartiality between peoples and princes. Italian unity would
be of great advantage to the Catholic religion and bring the
utmost glory to the Holy See. Of the Piedmontese and their
character. Of the House of Savoy, and eulogy thereof.
20 Connections and relationships of reigning families with the social
progress of peoples. Of the new dynasty which rules Piedmont
and the destiny which Providence has prepared for it.

> Table of contents of Vincenzo Gioberti's *Of the Moral
> and Civil Primacy of the Italians*, 1843, in D. Beales, *The
> Risorgimento and the Unification of Italy* (London, 1981)
> pp. 132–3.

(b) For Piedmont; against democracy

[The unitary solution] No nation has been less frequently united
in a single body than the Italian.... The dreamers say that one
25 can still achieve what hitherto has never been achieved.... But
this is childish, no more than the fantasy of rhetorical schoolboys,
two-a-penny poets, drawing-room politicians.... What would be
the pope's position in a kingdom of Italy? That of king? But this
is impossible, nobody even dreams of it. That of subject? But in
30 that case he would be dependent ...

[Federation] Confederations are the type of constitutions most
suited to Italy's nature and history.... The only obstacle to an
Italian confederation – a most serious obstacle – is foreign rule,
which penetrates deep into the peninsula. ... I maintain that an
35 Italian confederation is neither desirable nor possible if a foreign
power forms part of it; and that it would perhaps be desirable, but
so difficult as to be impossible without a foreign power ...

[Princes] At the present time the fact is that all power is in the hands of the princes. But this does not mean that everybody else
40 has only a minimal part to play. There is no such danger; it is not a minimal part for the following reason: the moment the actions of princes move from the plane of ideas to that of facts, they become the actions of the nation. If the peoples can do nothing without the princes, the princes can do nothing without the
45 peoples, they are not princes except in so far as they make their peoples act ...

[Democracy] To tell the truth, although a democratic conflagration is much threatened and feared in our days, it seems to me improbable, given the progress of our present democracy. ... In
50 some cases democracy is tyrannical and so estranges every other class; in other cases it subjects itself to the aristocracy; in most cases it disappears within the great class of educated persons. ... A democratic conflagration may continue for some time to be the fear of the police and the hope of secret societies. But it cannot
55 enter into any assessment of the foreseeable future, it cannot be an element to be calculated as an important undertaking. ...

[Savoy] The peace of Utrecht in 1714 founded a new kingdom in Italy for that worthy house of Savoy which had upheld the sacred fire of Italian virtue for the last century and a half. ...
60 During the eighteenth century, up to '89, not a single state was eliminated, there were only exchanges of towns, amalgamations of provinces, at one state's expense in favour of another. But one should note that all these joining together of lands were in favour of the monarchy of Savoy, which in the course of the century
65 increased by a third in population and almost doubled in territory. Equally notable is the method by which these additions were acquired, all at the expense of the house of Austria, and yet for the most part by fighting for them. Should such an example be imitated in similar natural conditions, or should it be avoided because the times have changed? One can only decide on each occasion ...

Cesare Balbo in 1844, from S. J. Woolf, *The Italian Risorgimento* (London, 1969) pp. 45–6.

70 **(c)** *Federation*

The dream of many people, but still a dream, is that a single law for all Italy can be improvised by the wave of a magic wand. No! For many generations in Turin, Parma, Rome,
75 Naples, Sicily, signed contracts and customary rights based on ancient and modern laws will continue. ... The result is that men cannot easily be detached from their natural centres. Whoever ignores this love of the individual patria in Italy will always build on sand. ...

80   Two states alone, the American and the Swiss federations, have
       shown even in these troubled years how to rule without contin-
       ual use of a standing army and hence without immense expense.
       The fact is that not only do they rest on the spontaneous, and
       continuously renewed consensus of the masses, but – while
85   reserving to the federal authority everything of common interest
       – they leave to all their peoples the enjoyment of their special
       rights, the leadership of the men they trust, the practice of their
       traditional and spontaneous ideas, a just pride in their sovereignty,
       which is as dear to peoples as to rulers. Hence the general struc-
90   ture does not invade the local structure; it does not humiliate,
       dishearten, harass; it does not sow resentment, it does not impose
       itself by the weight of a stolid force, it does not waste capital, it
       does not bleed families.

       Carlo Cattaneo, 1836, in S. J. Woolf, *The Italian
       Risorgimento* (London, 1969) pp. 50–1.

(d) *The future in the masses*

       I believe that socialism alone – not the French systems which
95   are all full of that monarchical and despotic idea which pre-
       vails in that nation, but the socialism expressed by the
       formula *Liberty and Association* [Mazzini's motto] – is the one
       not too distant future of Italy, and perhaps of Europe ... I am
       convinced that railways, telegraphs, industrial improvements,
100   commercial facilities, machines, etc. etc., by an inevitable
       economic law, increase the product, so long as its division is
       based on competition, but always increase it among very few
       hands and impoverish the multitude. Thus this boasted
       progress is nothing but regression. And if it wants to be con-
105   sidered as progress, this can only be in the sense that, by
       increasing the oppression of the plebs, it will drive them to a
       terrible revolution which, by immediately changing the
       entire social order, will turn what at the moment is the profit
       of the few into the profit of all. I am convinced that Italy
110   will be free and great or else a slave. I am convinced that the
       necessary remedies, such as a constitutional regime,
       Lombardy, Piedmont, etc. etc., far from drawing Italy nearer
       her Risorgimento, are driving her further away ...
           It will be a disaster if the plebs content themselves with vain
115   promises and so make their own fate depend on the will of
       others! ... Propaganda of ideas is a chimera, the education of
       people is an absurdity. Ideas come from facts, not facts from
       ideas, and the people will not be free when it is educated, but
       it will be educated when it is free.

       Carlo Pisacane, in S. J. Woolf, *The Italian Risorgimento*
       (London, 1969) pp. 58–9.

4 Early abortive risings

(a) *A conservative analysis*

The settlement imposed on Italy by the Congress of Vienna was as arbitrary as it was defective. It was based on no principle, not even that of legitimacy – as may be seen in the treatment given to Genoa and Venice. Certainly it was not based on
5 national interests or popular will. ... Hence the unfortunate risings of 1820 and 1821 [which] were easily suppressed, because the upper classes were divided and the masses took only a feeble part; nonetheless they had deplorable consequences for Italy. The governments of the country, without becoming
10 tyrannical, were thereby aroused to an extreme distrust of any idea of nationality. ... Time was beginning to efface the fatal traces of 1821, when the revolution of July 1830 in France shook the European social structure to its foundations. The repercussions of this great popular movement were widespread
15 in Italy. ... The movements organised after 1830, with one exception where peculiar administrative conditions applied, were easily suppressed even before they had broken out. Inevitably so; for these movements, relying solely upon republican ideas and demagogic passions, were sterile. A democratic
20 revolution has no chance of success in Italy. ... Active power resides almost exclusively in the middle class and part of the upper class, both of which groups have ultra-conservative inter-

ests to defend. ... The subversive doctrines of Young Italy are
therefore taking little hold among those who have an interest in
25 maintaining social order. Excepting the young, whose experience has not yet modified the doctrines imbibed in the exciting
atmosphere of the schools, only a tiny number of Italians exist
who are seriously supposed to apply the exalted principles of
that unfortunate and embittered sect ...
30 The history of the last thirty years, as well as an analysis of
the various elements in Italian society, will prove that military
or democratic revolutions can have little success in Italy. All
true friends of the country must therefore reject such means as
useless. They must recognise that they cannot truly help their
35 fatherland except by gathering in support of legitimate mon-
archs who have their roots deep in the national soil.

> From a book review by C. Cavour, May 1846, in
> D. Mack Smith, *The Making of Italy, 1796–1866*
> (London, 1988) pp. 105–6, 108.

Questions

a Why should the mention of Genoa by this particular
   writer be surprising (line 4)?

★ b Which secret society was supposed to be behind the
   risings of 1820 and 1831? Which was the one exception
   to the string of easy suppressions (line16)?

c Why did Cavour discount Young Italy?

d Which of the nationalist writers in the previous section
   would Cavour be most likely to support?

e Who might Cavour have been hoping to influence by
   this piece?

II   The Successes of 1848

Introduction

There is little doubt that the election of Pius IX in 1846 set in motion the liberal reforms which many Italian governments adopted, more or less unwillingly, over the next few years. Although the Pope soon came to regret his initial actions as opening a Pandora's box, the way these moves were interpreted by the rest of Italy transformed him into the nationalists' hero.

Open rebellion against the Austrians had to wait until the wave of European revolutions of 1848 had reached Vienna and dislodged Metternich. The moment that news reached Italy in mid-March the peoples of Milan and Venice rose up and ejected the Austrian garrisons. Piedmont then declared war; Naples and Tuscany followed suit; and for a few months all the Italian states, including the Papal States, were engaged against the Austrians.

The main question concerns Piedmont's role. What explained the tardy intervention? Was Charles Albert hustled into declaring himself; or, like the secret nationalist some thought he was, did he always intend to aid the insurgents but was merely preparing his ground? There were further doubts at the time about the fate of Lombardy and Venice. Some argued they should be incorporated into Piedmont, recognising Charles Albert as their monarch, in order to create a strong single unit. Republicans naturally protested at this, while federalists feared the two northern provinces would simply feed an insatiably expansionist Piedmont, swallowing, as the contemporary phrase went, Italian states like an artichoke, leaf by leaf.

In the south the difficulty was the older question of Sicily's independence. Palermo had been the first area to rebel in 1848 – even anteceding Paris – and was soon indicating its radical separatist demands.

1   Election of Pius IX: the system cracks

(a) *Pius IX signals a change of policy*

The affection that our good subjects have shown toward Us, and the incessant tokens of veneration that the Holy See has, in our

Person, received from them, have persuaded Us, that We may pardon them [political prisoners] without danger to the public at large. We accordingly determine and command, that the opening of our Pontificate be signalised by the following acts of sovereign clemency... . To all our subjects now actually in a place of punishment for political offenses, We remit the remainder of their sentences ... all our subjects who have quitted our dominions for political reasons may return to them ...

> Amnesty granted by Pius IX, 16 July 1846, from
> D. Mack Smith, *The Making of Italy, 1796–1866*
> (London, 1988) p. 116.

(b) *Mazzini appeals to the Pope*

There is no man, I will not say in Italy but in Europe more powerful than you. You have, therefore, most blessed father, immense duties; God measures them in accordance with the means which he gives to his creatures. Europe is in a tremendous crisis of doubts and of desires. Through the passage of time, aggravated by your predecessors and the exalted hierarchy of the Church, beliefs are dead; catholicism is lost in despotism: protestantism is losing itself in anarchy... . To fulfil the mission which God entrusts to you two things are necessary: to believe and to unify Italy. Without the first you will fall by the wayside, abandoned by God and by men; without the second you will not have that lever with which, alone, you can achieve great, holy, and enduring things.

> Open letter from Mazzini to Pius IX, 8 September
> 1847, quoted in E. E. Y. Hales, *Pio Nono* (London,
> 1956) p. 66.

(c) *Metternich pronounces on the new Pope*

Each day the Pope shows himself more lacking in any practical sense. Born and brought up in a *liberal* family, he has been formed in a bad school; a good priest, he has never turned his mind towards matters of government. Warm of heart and weak of intellect, he has allowed himself to be taken and ensnared, since assuming the tiara, in a net from which he no longer knows how to disentangle himself, and if matters follow their natural course, he will be driven out of Rome... . A *liberal* Pope is not a possibility. A Gregory VII could become the master of the world, a Pius IX cannot become that. He can destroy, but he cannot build. What the Pope has already destroyed by his liberalism is his own temporal power; what he is unable to destroy is his spiritual power; it is that power which will cancel the harm done by his worthless counsellors. But to what dangerous conflicts have not these men exposed

the man and the cause they wanted to serve.... The veil is lib-
40 eralism; it will disappear in Italy, as in every other country,
before radicalism in action.

> Metternich to Austrian agents in Paris and Milan,
> October and December 1847, in E. E. Y. Hales, *Pio
> Nono* (London, 1956) pp. 67–8.

Questions

a   What was the Holy See? Define temporal power and
spiritual power. In extract (c) explain 'assuming the tiara'
(line 29).

b   What does extract (b) tell you about Mazzini's methods
of persuasion? What would have been the Pope's likely
reaction?

★ c   Were Metternich's predictions of (i) the fate of Pius
IX, (ii) the development of liberalism into radicalism,
confirmed by events in 1848–9?

★ d   What justification do these passages prove for the view
that Pius' election was a watershed in the history of the
Risorgimento?

(d) *Liberal hopes of the King of Piedmont*

At that time the King was a mystery; and although his later
conduct has been plainly intelligible, he will perhaps remain
partly a mystery, even for history. At that time, the principal
events of his life, those of 1821 and 1833, were certainly not
5   in his favour: no one could reconcile his grand ideas for
Italian independence with the Austrian marriages ... his
inclination to aggrandize the House of Savoy with his court-
ing of the Jesuits ... his display of piety and his old-woman-
ish penances with the loftiness of thought and firmness of
10 character demanded by bold enterprises.
    No one, therefore, trusted Carlo Alberto. A great evil for a
ruler in his circumstances. Trying to keep the support of the
two parties by guile, you end by losing that of both ...
    I told him at length of the disgust of all honest, sensible
15 men at the Mazzinian foolishness and wickedness; of the
suggestion made that I should start to do something or other
to try to give a new and better direction to the people's
activities; of the excellent disposition I had found, with few
exceptions, wherever I went. I continued as follows:
20   'Your Majesty, I have never belonged to any secret society;
I have had nothing to do with intrigues and plots; but as I

have spent my childhood and youth in various parts of Italy so that all are acquainted with me, they know I am no spy and therefore no one distrusts me; I have, therefore, known
25 about their secret affairs just as though I had been one of them. They still tell me everything, and I think I can assure you, without fear of deceiving myself, that the majority of them recognise the absurdity of what has hitherto happened and want to change their policy. All are persuaded that
30 without force nothing can be done; that the only force in Italy is that of Piedmont; but that they cannot count even on this as long as Europe is peaceful and organised as at present ...'

I stopped and awaited the reply, which, to judge by the
35 King's expression, did not seem likely to be hostile. But I guessed that, in regard to the essential, it was likely to be sibylline, and that it would not leave one any the wiser. Instead, he said quietly but firmly, without any hesitation or turning his glance away, but looking me straight in the eyes:
40 'Let those gentlemen know that they should remain quiet and take no steps now, as nothing can be done at present; but they can rest assured that when the opportunity arises, *my life, my children's lives, my arms, my treasure, my army, all shall be given in the cause of Italy.*'
45 Expecting something quite different, I remained for a moment speechless. I almost thought I had not heard aright.

> Massimo D'Azeglio on his visit to King Charles Albert, October 1845, in D. Mack Smith, *The Making of Italy, 1796–1866* (London, 1988) pp. 111–14.

(e) *Hopes in Lombardy for Piedmont aid*

Events are being precipitated by the brutality of the police and the ferocity of Radetzky. Four months ago I could
50 never have believed that hatred could spread everywhere so fast... . The army of spies has been doubled. People live in continual fear of being arrested even on the slightest excuse. All hopes are concentrated on Piedmont. Charles Albert's name is now known even in country districts; and you can
55 imagine how I praise him wherever I can, directly or indirectly... . We rely upon Piedmont to save us, and you will find that every village in Lombardy, however small, is on your side. Even the Italian Tyrol is burning to join the common cause. It would now be impossible to prevent a
60 fight between Austrians and Italians, between slavery and the cause of national independence. We are at a terrifying crossroads, and it is your army and your King who must pull

us out of this agonising situation – your King whom we
hope shortly to hail as ours too, with all our heartfelt
65 gratitude.

> Luigi Torelli to Maurizio Farina, February 1848, in
> D. Mack Smith, *The Making of Italy, 1796–1866*
> (London, 1988) pp. 124–5.

(f) Charles Albert grants a constitution – the Statuto – for Piedmont

Article 1   The apostolic Roman Catholic religion is the only
religion of the state. Other cults now existing are tolerated, in
conformity with the law.

Article 2   The state is governed by a representative monarch
70 ical government. The throne is hereditary according to the
Salic law.

Article 3   The legislative power shall be exercised collectively
by the King and two houses, the Senate and the House of
Deputies ...

75 *Article 5*   To the King alone belongs the executive power ...

Article 6   The King appoints to all of the offices of the state,
and makes the necessary decrees and regulations for the execu-
tion of the laws ...

Article 10   The initiative in legislation shall belong both to the
80 King and the two houses. All bills, however, imposing taxes or
relating to the budget shall first be presented to the House of
Deputies ...

Article 28   The press shall be free, but the law may suppress
abuses of this freedom ...

85 *Article 29*   Property of all kinds whatsoever is inviolable ...

Article 30   No tax shall be levied or collected without the
consent of the houses and the approval of the King ...

Article 33   The Senate shall be composed of members who
have attained the age of forty years, appointed for life by the
90 King ...

Article 39   The elective house shall be composed of deputies
chosen by the electoral districts as provided by law ...

Article 68   Justice emanates from the King and shall be
administered in his name by the judges whom he appoints.

> *Statuto*, 4 March 1848, in D. Mack Smith, *The Making of
> Italy, 1796–1866* (London, 1988) pp. 136–9.

★ *a* In extract (d) why were Charles Albert's roles in 1821 and 1833 'not in his favour' (lines 4–5)?

★ *b* How reliable is D'Azeglio's assertion that he never belonged to any secret society? What were these 'intrigues and plots'?

c Why did D'Azeglio expect 'something quite different' (line 45)?

d Account for the changing expectations of Charles Albert in extracts (d) and (e).

e In extract (e) who was Radetzky (line 49)?

f In extract (f) explain 'representative monarchical government' (lines 69–70). How did this constitution differ from the British system?

g Which articles of the *Statuto* retained power for the Crown; which would have pleased the liberals; and which were left deliberately vague?

h Do these documents fully explain why the Piedmontese constitution was granted?

2   The revolution begins

(a) *Risings in the south*

[November 1847] To show the general satisfaction at this event [a change of ministry], and to push the King to greater things, such as joining the Italian customs league that was being formed between Rome, Tuscany and Piedmont, it was decided to mount
5   a public demonstration; and, to hearten the timid, this took place at night ... the cry went up: 'Long live Italy, long live Pius IX, long live the customs league, long live the King.' ... [December 1847] In the royal palace the King did nothing but discuss police matters ... he frequently cursed Pius IX who had disturbed the
10   hornet's nest, and expressed contempt for the weakness of Leopold [of Tuscany] and Charles Albert; mounting his high horse, he would say: 'I'll go and be a colonel in Russia or Austria rather than Yield and show weakness.' ...

[the author then left Naples and returned on 7 February 1848] As
15   the boat entered the harbour and prepared to anchor, I saw several ships with tricolor flags, in one of which was my brother Peppino, who shouted to me across the water: 'Constitution, amnesty ... everything is changed, disembark, disembark.' I embraced him and asked him: 'How has all this come about?' 'There was a great demon-
20   stration on 27 January [1848], and on the 29th was published the royal decree promising a constitution, and giving a full amnesty.' Was so much extracted by shouting?' In Naples there has been shouting

but in Palermo a terrible revolution which has defeated the troops, and a revolution in Cilento.' 'And Ferdinand, who would rather be a colonel in Russia than yield, has yielded?' 'Yes, and as he signed the constitutional decree do you know what he said? "Don Pio Nono and Carlo Alberto wanted to trip me up with a stick, so I'll try this girder on them. Now let's all enjoy ourselves as best we can." ...' ...
Soon people were awaiting the constitution with impatience. Bozzelli was compiling it by command of the king. Everyone imagined it as he wanted it himself, and some hastily wrote and printed proposals for a constitution, and hawked them about, and gave them to you to read, and asked: 'Will it do?' Old men said there was no need for a new constitution. That of 1820 would suffice, with a few slight modifications, thus affirming that the rights of the nation had never lapsed. This was the idea of the Sicilians, who were only interested in having the Constitution of 1812 brought up to date, but by Parliament and not by the King. On 10 February the King accepted the Constitution, on the 11th it was published.... The Constitution was [virtually] a copy, or rather translation, of the French charter of 1830. Bozzelli thought he had written the laws of Solon, which would immortalise him and make the people very happy.

> L. Settembrini's memoirs, 1879, in D. Beales, *The Risorgimento and the Unification of Italy* (London, 1981) pp. 145–7.

(b) *Radetzky loses Milan*

March 18–19　　Some days ago I had various information that an attempt at insurrection would be made in Milan on March 18. On the evening of the seventeenth, news arrived by telegraph from Vienna of the generous concessions made by His Majesty, and today notices about it were up at every street corner. I hoped that this would have calmed Milan. The Vice-Governor, Count O'Donnell, begged me not to use armed force against the citizenry unless requested by the civil authorities.

Toward midday I was informed that people were gathering at various points and that schoolchildren were being fetched home by their parents. The armed forces were in their barracks because an outbreak of revolt seemed so improbable. I was in my office when the storm broke out and had to flee to the citadel so as to escape being surrounded by the mob. Increasingly alarming news soon began to come in ...

By this time fighting had broken out at various places. There was shooting from windows, and all sorts of objects were thrown from the rooftops. Many a brave soldier lost his life in this way. When General Rath moved his troops into the centre to occupy the Piazza del Duomo and the main government buildings, there was tough fighting in the streets, but the soldiers got through despite the barricades.

65   At this point I was handed proclamations from a Provisional Government set up in the town hall. Amongst other things, a National Guard had been established.... Our losses in dead and wounded I do not know, but they cannot be small. For the moment, all is calm, but possibly fighting will start again at dawn.

70   I am determined to remain master of Milan whatever happens. If the fighting does not stop, I shall bombard the city... .

March 21, 10 a.m... . The revolutionary party is moving with a caution and cleverness which make it obvious that they are being directed by military officers from abroad... .

75   My information from the provinces, though slight, is very alarming, for the whole country is in revolt and even the peasants are armed... .

At nine o'clock the news spread that the Piedmontese army had deployed along the Ticino and that groups of volunteers

80   had already crossed the river... .

March 22 It is the most frightful decision of my life, but I can no longer hold Milan. The whole country is in revolt. I am pressed in the rear by the Piedmontese ... I shall withdraw toward Lodi to avoid the large towns and while the countryside is still open.

Field Marshall Radetzky to Austrian Minister, 18–22 March 1848, in D. Mack Smith, *The Making of Italy, 1796–1866* (London, 1988) pp. 141–5.

Questions

a   In extract (a) who is the king being cheered (line 6)? Who are 'Don Pio Nono' and 'Carlo Alberto'? What is the significance of the tricolour flags? Why should the king have chosen Russia or Austria (lines 12–13)?

b   From which country did the Italians adopt the notion of a customs league?

c   In extract (a) explain Ferdinand's metaphor (lines 26–8).

★ *d*   What were the differences between the constitutions of 1812 (in Sicily), 1820 and 1848. What is the writer's attitude to this constitution making in 1848?

★ *e*   Why should it have been ironic that the Neapolitan constitution, published on 11 February 1848, was a copy of the French in 1830?

f   In extract (b) what were the concessions from Vienna, which arrived on 17 March 1848? Why did these not placate the Milanese?

g   To what forces and agents does Radetzky attribute his defeat in Milan? How reliable is his judgement?

h   From these extracts what were the essential differences between the national movements in Naples and Milan?

3   The rising in Venice

(a) *Prices*

In 1845 the Venetian harvest was poor, with heavy rain and floods being mainly responsible. A year later only the maize crop was reported as being normal, with wheat scarce and potatoes blighted completely. These setbacks were not as
5 serious as in other parts of the empire, such as Bohemia and Silesia, but the Venetian situation was greatly aggravated by the extensive exporting of cereals, particularly maize. As a result prices rocketed. In 1845 the average wholesale price in Venice for a Venetian bushel of wheat was 16.22 Austrian lire, much
10 the same as it had been ever since 1819. In 1846 this average price rose to 18.56 Au. lire, and in the first months of 1847 it leapt to 31.92 Au. lire. A similar catastrophic rise is to be found for maize ... The price indexes for the provincial markets reveal an almost identical pattern... .
15 From all over the Veneto in the early months of 1847 reports flooded in to the central authorities of the peasants' suffering... . In some areas desperation turned to violence ... [these incidents] appear trifling when compared with the contemporary large-scale revolts in the heartlands of the Austrian
20 empire... . But the Venetian peasantry was not noted for its militancy, and widespread disturbances of this sort had not been reported since the famine years of 1816–17 ...

In the cities the situation was equally critical. Crop failures meant the destruction of home demand for manufactured
25 goods, and the general European commercial depression of 1846–47 took its toll in the Venetian cities as elsewhere... .

The Austrians' reaction during the first months of 1847 was of crucial importance, for the impression they gave was one of the both callousness and incompetence... . They had not
30 reduced taxation, prevented the export of maize, or supplied sufficient employment... . In general, the disaffection of the Veneto from Austrian rule dates from these first months of 1847... .

[in January and February 1848] maize prices had returned to
35 normal [but] those for wheat remained well above the average ... a Venetian bushel of wheat still cost between 19.50 and 21.50 Au. Lire.

> P. Ginsborg, *Daniele Manin and the Venetian Revolution of 1848–49* (Cambridge, 1979) pp. 59–64, 74.

(b) *Opera plays its part*

The police, perhaps already alarmed by the political enthusiasm aroused by *Nabucco*, seem to have found in the crusade

40 preached by the pope [in *I Lombardi*] an allegory of the proposal, recently put forward, to unite the Italian states under the
aegis of the pope ... *I Lombardi* stirred Italian patriotic feeling
even more deeply than *Nabucco* with its fullblooded tunes and
its romantic glorification of Lombardy's ancient military fame.
45 The chorus 'O Signore dal tetto natio' aroused the kind of
fervour that 'Land of our Fathers' creates at a gathering of
Welshmen ...

The Italian public, however, took *Ernani* to its heart, once
more identifying itself with the outlawed hero, sharing in the
50 stage conspiracy against his oppressor, and substituting for
'Carlo Quinto' in the chorus ... the name of Pio Nono ...

Attila, produced in Venice during the carnival of 1846, had a
greater success, not on account of its dramatic or musical supe-
riority, but because it contained, besides other patriotic senti-
55 ments which echoed the aspiration of a resurgent nation, the
line 'Take the whole universe, but leave Italy to me'. A more
parochial patriotism was aroused by the presentation of the
founding of Venice, 'mother of great men and brave'.

D. Hussey, *Verdi* (London, 1940) pp. 34–5, 38, 43.

(c) *Manin proclaims a republic in Venice*

We are free, and we have a double right to boast of it
60 because we have become free without shedding a drop of
blood, either our own or our brothers', for I call all men
brothers. But it is not enough to have overthrown the old
government; we must put another in its place. The right
one, I think, is the republic. It will remind us of our past
65 glories improved by modern liberties. We do not thereby
mean to separate ourselves from our Italian brothers. Rather
we will form one of those centres which must bring about
the gradual fusion of Italy into one. *Viva la Repubblica! Viva
la libertà! Viva San Marco!*

Daniele Manin, 22 March 1848, in P. Ginsborg, *Daniele
Manin and the Venetian Revolution of 1848–49*
(Cambridge, 1979) p. 101.

(d) *Venetian republican programme*

70 No communism – No social subversion – No government in
the Piazza – Respect for property – Equality for all in the face
of the law – Full liberty of thought and deed – Free discussion
without tumults – Improvement of the condition of those poor
who wish to live from their work.

Summary by Gustavo Modena, 29 March 1848, in
P. Ginsborg, *Daniele Manin and the Venetian Revolution of
1848–49* (Cambridge, 1979) p. 115.

4   Piedmont intervenes

(a)   *The official declaration*

... Peoples of Lombardy and Venetia, our arms, which were concentrating on your frontier when you forestalled events by liberating your glorious Milan, are now coming to offer you in the latter phases of your fight the help which a brother expects
5   from a brother, and a friend from a friend.

We will support your just desires, confident as we are in the help of that God who is manifestly on our side; of the God who has given Pius IX to Italy; of God whose helpful hand has wonderfully enabled Italy to rely on her own strength.
10   In order to show more openly our feelings of Italian brotherhood, we have ordered our troops as they move into Lombardy and Venice to carry the Cross of Savoy imposed on the tricolor flag of Italy.

> Charles Albert's proclamation to Lombardy and Venice, 23 March 1848, in D. Mack Smith, *The Making of Italy, 1796–1866* (London, 1988) p. 148.

(b)   *Unofficial reasons*

The die is cast today, and I enclose Charles Albert's proclama-
15   tion (if you have not already seen it) which will prove that we are moving into Lombardy. 'After the fighting is all over,' some

cynics will say! But the phrase would be unfair, because after the fighting will come diplomacy and the treaty-making, and here our strength will count. In any case it is a matter of life
20 and death for us, and I think our action will give us good hopes of increasing Piedmontese territory.

The King was quite admirable, and it was his view that carried the cabinet. He said the state would be lost if we did not fight. Perhaps in declaring war he might be risking his
25 throne, but he was ready for that.

> P. Pinelli to Gioberti, 23 March 1848, in D. Mack Smith, *The Making of Italy, 1796–1866* (London, 1988) p. 147.

Questions

a   In extract (a) what is Charles Albert implying by the phrase 'when you forestalled events'? What is the significance of the new flag?

b   In extract (b) if it was 'a matter of life and death', why did Charles Albert hesitate so long before committing himself?

c   How do these two extracts differ over motives for Piedmontese intervention? Explain the differences.

---

5   Suspicions amongst the Alliance

(a) *Palermo versus Naples*

The gravest preoccupation for all was Sicily, which rejected the Neapolitan Constitution of February 10, and replied that it still wanted its own Constitution of 1812 … desiring to be an entirely separate and independent Kingdom, with a Viceroy who
5 should be either a royal prince or a Sicilian citizen and should have the fullest powers; that the ministers should be nominated by the King but operate in Palermo, that there should be no more Neapolitan troops in Sicily, and that for affairs common to the two Kingdoms there should be established a mixed commis-
10 sion chosen from among the members of both Parliaments. These conditions seemed harsh not only to the King, but to a good many Neapolitans and Italians, who said and put in print that Sicily, in separating herself from Naples, would separate herself from Italy; that this 'Sicilianism' was unworthy, an ancient
15 rancour between Palermo and Naples, the metropolis of the whole Kingdom; that brother nations ought to unite under the similar laws and institutions which produce similar customs and sentiments; that two constitutions would separate the two peoples

more than the sea and for ever; that the Constitution of February
20 10 had been granted not on account of the shouts of Naples but
of the blood of Palermo, and that they should accept it as their
conquest. The Sicilians replied that they were not separating
themselves from Italy, that their independence did no harm to
Italy, which ought to unite as a federation and not into one
25 Kingdom; that they had never lost their constitution since people
never lose their rights, and now they had won it back with blood
and not with shouts; that if Naples was a sister rather than a
master, there would be no more rancour, no more occasion for
hatred; that they knew the Bourbon and wanted none of the
30 good that came from him; that they never wanted to see again in
Sicily those dear brother Neapolitans who had bombarded their
cities ...

[The writer continues] War against Austria was holy and
necessary. But to want Ferdinand II to make that war was
35 madness. To believe that he could be forced to make it was stu-
pidity... . Either we had to remain Neapolitans, and not think
of Italy, and be content with the Constitution of February 10
without going any further. Or, if we wanted to fight Austria,
we had to broaden the Constitution and chase out Ferdinand,
40 or at least take from him all the power he had over the army
and leave him only the name of King.

> L. Settembrini's memoirs, 1879, in D. Beales, *The
> Risorgimento and the Unification of Italy* (London, 1981)
> pp. 147–9.

Questions

a Explain the term 'Viceroy' (line 4). Who is 'the
   Bourbon' (line 29)?
b Is it possible to tell whether the writer supports the
   Neapolitan or Sicilian viewpoint?
c What does the phrase 'broaden the Constitution' mean
   (line 39)? In what way does Settembrini feel the
   revolution was caught in the middle?

(b) Milan versus Turin

Today the King told me about the meeting with his generals:
they are extremely annoyed with the state of opinion in
Lombardy, and national feeling in Piedmont is becoming really
alarmed.
5   Tell me my friend, frankly and in confidence, what do you
think Piedmont has to gain by focusing with Lombardy? She
may be losing her existing primacy and all its attendant

advantages just to become a secondary planet in a different
universe. Only posterity will do justice to the blindness of
10 your Lombards. Past experience teaches them nothing. The
generous and disinterested Piedmontese nation, with massive
and almost unprecedented enthusiasm, is sacrificing her
blood, her money, and almost her position of primacy to
support her brothers; and yet, just when we could make one
15 single family, here she is received like a predatory foe! This,
my dear Casati, is too much. The only talk at Milan appar-
ently is of a republic; and they even want Genoa to go
republican too… . If after so much heroic effort, if after proclaiming ourselves a nation to the whole of Europe, we then
20 divide into as many tiny states and republics as there are
cities and municipal rivalries, and if we are then swallowed
up or beaten by the foreigner, we shall have left a fine page
of history!

> Count di Castagnetto to Mayor of Milan, 16 April
> 1848, in D. Mack Smith, *The Making of Italy,
> 1796–1866* (London, 1988) pp. 149–50.

(c) *Florence versus Turin*

If we are not mistaken, Sicily must already have proclaimed a
25 republican government and at Naples there must shortly be a
revolution. Genoa will only wait a few days before imitating
her sister Venice. We democrats and republicans are laying
plans for our own country… . Above all else do not allow
yourselves, in the name of God, to be deceived by Charles
30 Albert and the princes – hold firm and you will triumph. We
are all waiting anxiously to see what Milan will decide. God
prevent the Milanese … throwing themselves into the arms
of those who now wish to profit from the fruit of their
heroic sacrifices… . But whatever happens, if Venice holds
35 firm, Italy will be saved.

> R. Berlinghieri from Florence to Manin, 27 March
> 1848, in P. Ginsborg, *Daniele Manin and the Venetian
> Revolution of 1848–49* (Cambridge, 1979) p. 145.

(d) *Milan versus Venice*

Here the proclamation of the republic at Venice has aroused
displeasure. Everyone fears that Venice wants to detach itself
from the Italian family so as to return to the particularism of
the republic of St Mark … the republic is desired by every-
40 one … but this government could not and must not declare
it. The Sardinian troops would not have marched into our
territory to throw the common enemy out of Italy if they
had been summoned by a republican government. Charles

Albert loves his throne too much, and we need the
45 Piedmontese troops.

> J. Pezzato from Milan to Manin, 28 March 1848, in
> P. Ginsborg, *Daniele Manin and the Venetian Revolution
> of 1848–49* (Cambridge, 1979) p. 145.

Questions

a In extract (b) why is Genoese talk of a republic particularly threatening to Piedmont?

b Explain 'disinterested Piedmontese nation' (line 11).

c In extract (b) how would Castagnetto define his 'nation' (line 19)? What were its envisaged boundaries? What was the institutional framework?

d In extract (c) who are the princes (line 30)?

★ e How accurate was the writer in extract (c) in his prediction of events for Sicily, Naples and Genoa? Who are 'those who now wish to profit' (line 33)?

f In extract (d) where is the desired republic (line 39)?

g What do extracts (b), (c) and (d) suggest is the preferred form of government by the Milanese people. Which of these extracts is least reliable on this point? How do you account for the different attitude expressed in extract (f), section 1 of this chapter?

h Account for the different attitude towards Piedmont from all these extracts.

III   The Failures of 1848–9

Introduction

Just as it could be said that Pope Pius IX was largely responsible for the start of the nationalist movement in the 1840s, so too was he the first to signal his abandonment. His Allocution of 29 April 1848, condemning the war against Austria, came as a thunderbolt to all alike. The resulting confusion certainly helped the King of Naples to force through a counter-revolution the next month and also withdraw from the war.

Piedmont persisted with the campaign. Its critics, however, charged it with being more concerned about extending its aegis (and actual territory) over Lombardy and Venetia than in freeing the Italian people. After much hesitation these two regions did agree to fuse with Piedmont to create a Kingdom of North Italy. This development came too late to prevent Piedmont's defeat by the Austrians at Custoza in July. Charles Albert concluded an armistice and returned Lombardy to Austria; but he had not given up the prospect of continuing the war at a later date. In March 1849 Piedmont attacked the Austrians again, only to be decisively defeated within a number of days. Properly mortified, the King abdicated, to be succeeded by his son, Victor Emmanuel.

That left the struggle to be continued by the Republics of Venice and Rome. The latter had been formed in early 1849 after radicals had seized power and the Pope fled from the city. Mazzini quickly arrived and established himself as the dominant leader – to give the lie to those who divorce intellectual theorists from men of action. Historians have disagreed over his eventual aims. Using the unorthodox talents of Garibaldi, the new Republic resisted attacks for some time before submitting to the French in July 1849. Next month Venice surrendered to the Austrians.

1   The rulers react

(a) *Papal repudiation*

Nor are there wanting men who thus speak of Us, as though We had been the especial authors of the public commotions which

had recently occurred, not only in other parts of Europe, but likewise in Italy... . We at the outset, not stimulated by encour-
5   agements or advice, but prompted by our own singular affection toward the people placed under the temporal dominion of the Church, granted more large indulgence to those who had departed from their duty of allegiance to the pontifical govern-ment; and We subsequently made speed to adopt certain mea-
10 sures, which We had judged conducive in themselves to the prosperity of that people ...

Seeing that some at present desire that We too, along with the other princes of Italy and their subjects, should engage in war against the Austrians, We have thought it convenient to proclaim
15 clearly and openly, in this our solemn assembly, that such a measure is altogether alien from our counsels, inasmuch as We, albeit unworthy, are upon earth as viceregent of Him that is the Author of Peace and Lover of Charity, and, conformably to the function of our supreme apostolate, We reach to and embrace all
20 kindreds, peoples, and nations, with equal solicitude of paternal affection. But if, notwithstanding, there are not wanting among our subjects those who allow themselves to be carried away by the example of the rest of the Italians, in what manner could we possibly curb their ardour?
25 And in this place We cannot refrain from repudiating, before the face of all nations, the treacherous advice, published moreover in journals, and in various works, of those who would have the Roman Pontiff to be the head and to preside over the formation of some sort of novel republic of the whole Italian people.
30 Rather, on this occasion, moved hereto by the love We bear them, We do urgently warn and exhort the said Italian people to abstain with all diligence from the like counsels, deceitful and ruinous to Italy herself, and to abide in close attachment to their respective sovereigns, of whose good will they have already had
35 experience, so as never to let themselves be torn away from the obedience they owe them.

Allocution of Pius IX, 29 April 1848, in L. C. Farini, *The Roman State, 1815–50* (London, 1851–4) II, pp. 106–11.

(b) *Counter coup at Naples*

[The republican party], seeing the failure of all its efforts at the different points where it had sought to carry its ideas into practice, and believing the ground best prepared at
40 Naples, mounted the coup of May 15... . What were the consequences? That his Sicilian Majesty, who required only a pretext to enable him to recall the force of 15 or 20,000 men which he had sent against his will to fight in the plains of Venetia, quickly seized on the coup and summoned them

45 back, declaring that ... , threatened ... by internal enemies, he could not help other Italian Powers in their struggle against the foreign oppressor ...

As for the retrogades, they deserve scarcely more indulgence, for they also have gravely compromised by their intrigues the
50 highest interests of Order.... . Their most active centres are Rome and Turin.... . It is they who skilfully put doubt and uncertainty into an august conscience, and in a manner dictated the publication, which at the moment when they least expected it, gave such powerful aid to the Austrians. It is they also, who using the
55 scattered members of a certain Congregation, have neglected nothing to neutralise the efforts which the Piedmontese Ministry has been making to prosecute the war vigorously.

> Dispatches of the Belgian envoy in Rome, 19 September 1848, in D. Beales, *The Risorgimento and the Unification of Italy* (London, 1981), p. 143.

(c) *A dyspeptic overview*

When the other Italian rulers saw that the war was just designed to increase the power of this rival [Piedmont] who might
60 threaten their existence, they began deserting the cause. The Bourbon King of Naples first set the example: he intrigued, corrupted, disarmed the citizens of Naples by deceit, and recalled those of his troops who had gone to fight Austria. The Pope and the Grand Duke of Tuscany were capable only of secret, though
65 systematic, opposition; but what they most feared in the world was the reappearance of a large kingdom in northern Italy.

> Carlo Pisacane, 1850–1, in D. Mack Smith, *The Making of Italy, 1796–1866* (London, 1988) pp. 157–8.

Questions

★ a Account for the Pope's defensive tone in the Allocution. What were the 'certain measures' (lines 9–10)? Which authors had published 'the treacherous advice' (line 26)?

b Why should the Pope's recommendation for Italians to be obedient to their respective sovereigns appear ironical for the Piedmontese?

c Why did the Pope condemn the war against the Austrians?

d In extract (b) what political grouping were the 'retrogrades'? What publication had they advised? Who were the members (line 55) who helped them?

e Compare the reasons given in these extracts for the Pope and the King of Naples deserting the *Risorgimento*.

2 The brief life and death of the kingdom of upper Italy

(a) *The price of Piedmontese assistance*

The minister of war has praised the generous sentiments of the king and his sons, but has made us note clearly that Piedmont cannot be inspired by a purely chivalrous spirit and awaits some recompense for its great sacrifices. He did not make it clear of
5 what this recompense should consist, but many of those close to the king have said openly that Piedmont and the Lombardy–Venetian kingdom should form a constitutional kingdom with its seat at Milan ... the fact is that the word 'republic' displeases him and his ministers, and also his troops,
10 who are realists in the most narrow sense... . From this you will see, citizen ministers, that our presence at the camp of the king is superfluous until Venice takes some definite resolution upon its political system and upon its union with, or independence from Lombardy. This resolution should be taken with all
15 possible haste because, in our opinion, until the king knows our intentions and those of the Lombards, the military effort will not proceed with that speed which you and all Italy require.

> Count Cittadella to Venetian government, 14 April 1848, in P. Ginsborg, *Daniele Manin and the Venetian Revolution of 1848–49* (Cambridge, 1979) p. 187.

(b) *Manin against fusion*

It is vital that the Italian states, in their composition and exten-
20 sion, should be based upon historical tradition. Peoples who have different origins and customs should not be forced together, because otherwise civil war will follow the war of independence. Finally, no state should be refused the republican form of government if it feels better suited to it than to the
25 transitional stage of a constitutional monarchy.

> D. Manin to a French friend, 7 June 1848, in P. Ginsborg, *Daniele Manin and the Venetian Revolution of 1848–49* (Cambridge, 1979) p. 226.

(c) *Conditional union advised for Venice*

Venice should therefore define very clearly the conditions on which she will yield. She should insist that a constituent assembly must meet to decide a new constitution. In particular she should insist that every alternative parliament will be
30 summoned to meet on her soil... . To be sure Venice and the Venetian lands have much to learn from Piedmont: habits of firm and regular administration, a more solid educational

system, and a broad-based foundation for the army. And
Piedmont in her turn can gain something from other parts of
35 Italy, so long as she seeks not to absorb Italy into herself but
to make herself more Italian. There are two main things that
Venetia and Lombardy can and should demand from
Piedmont, so that we may free all Italy as far as our furthest
linguistic frontiers, in other words up to and including Fruili
40 and what is called the Italian Tyrol. We should demand that
Piedmont unite herself with the other regions of Italy in a
confederation; and also that a national parliament be set up
in Rome in which common rights and duties should be dis-
cussed. It will be a sign of Piedmont's desire for fraternity if
45 generous and harmonious agreements between the south and
the north of Italy can thus be brought about.

> Speech composed (but never spoken) by Tommaseo for
> the Venice Assembly, 4 July 1848, in D. Mack Smith, *The
> Making of Italy, 1796–1866* (London, 1988) pp. 153–5.

(d) *Manin for fusion*

The enemy is at our gates, counting on our divisions. Let us
give him the lie. Let us forget all parties today. Let us show
that today we are neither royalists nor republicans but that
50 we are all citizens. To the republicans I say – the future is for
us. All that has been done or is being done is provisional.
The decision belongs to the Diet at Rome.

> D. Manin to Venetian Assembly, 4 July 1848, in
> P. Ginsborg, *Daniele Manin and the Venetian Revolution of
> 1848–49* (Cambridge, 1979) p. 250.

Questions

a What were the Piedmontese objectives and fears?
b In extract (b) what is implied by 'transitional stage'
   (line 25)?
c Why does Manin appear to give different advice in
   extracts (b) and (d)? Can the two statements be
   reconciled?
d In extract (c) what was a 'constituent assembly' (lines
   27–28)? In what way did Tommaseo hope to shackle
   Piedmont to the nationalist cause?
e Suggest reasons why his speech was never delivered.

(e) *Charles Albert explains the Salasco armistice, August 1848*

The enemy increased; my army was almost alone in the struggle. The want of provisions forced us to abandon the positions
we had conquered... . With my army I had retired to the
defence of Milan; but ... The interior defence of the town
5   could not be sustained ... The throbs of my heart were ever for
Italian independence, but Italy has not yet shown to the world
that she can conquer alone.

    People of the kingdom! Show yourselves strong in a *first*
misfortune... . Repose confidence in your King. The cause of
10 Italian independence is not yet lost.

> Proclamation by Charles Albert, 10 August 1848, in
> F. Eyck (ed.), *The Revolutions of 1848–49* (Edin-
> burgh, 1972) pp. 120–1.

(f) *The end of upper Italy*

The King [of Piedmont's] plan at first seemed about to
succeed. Not only Lombardy but even Venice and the Veneto
placed themselves in his hands. Though his real aim was conquest only up to the Mincio [i.e. without Venice], he pre-
15 tended to accept the Venetian offer ... in fact he had affected
to accept Venice merely so as to consolidate his hold over
Lombardy.

    The outlook then changed... . The Austrian Marshal then
emerged from Verona and broke through the thin line that
20 opposed his advance. Charles Albert attacked with part of his
army and was defeated [at Custoza, July 1848]; then, instead of
threatening the Austrians by consolidating behind the line of
the Po, he rushed to occupy Milan. After an insignificant skir-
mish he surrendered this city and retreated over the Ticino
25 amid the curses and stupefaction of the populace ...

    [in March 1849] Piedmont defied Austria again, yet
remained almost completely inactive. The army accepted battle
without any plan of campaign and without even a base. It met
predictable and irremediable defeat [at Novara]

> Carlo Pisacane, 1850–1, in D. Mack Smith, *The Making
> of Italy, 1796–1866* (London, 1988) pp. 158, 160.

(g) *Austrian view of Austrian terms to Piedmont*

30 The armistice conditions had already been given to the
Piedmontese general when I was told of Charles Albert's abdi-
cation during the night; and the fact was confirmed later by
the general himself.

    Because of the king's utter untrustworthiness, we had made
35 these conditions severe; yet since they had already been deliv-

ered, I decided not to call the general back but to await events. I thought that the new King Victor Emmanuel would want this severity mitigated, and was therefore quite prepared to grant some concessions in order to win his trust. What I
40 foresaw, happened ...

In the afternoon of the day before yesterday, the King also had a personal conversation with me at our advance posts. He frankly declared his firm intention of defeating the democratic Revolutionary Party, to which his father had latterly given
45 such free rein that it became a real threat to himself and his throne. He said he only needed a little time for this, but it was especially important for him to avoid being discredited at the outset of his reign, because otherwise he would not be able to find any suitable ministers. This was the principal reason why
50 he wanted the clause concerning the fort of Alessandria altered, because our occupation of the *whole* place – the only garrison town he possesses in Piedmont – would alienate the loyalty of the army, which he needs for the maintainance of his throne. Apart from this it would also alienate the people and
55 parliament.

There is so much truth in this point that I could not dispute it. I therefore consented, and consider that I was right in the matter. If we fail to win the confidence of the new King and if we do not help him to maintain his dignity, conditions in Piedmont will
60 afford us no guarantee whatsoever of peace in the future.

Field Marshal Radetzky to Prince Schwarzenberg, 26 March 1849, in D. Mack Smith, *The Making of Italy, 1796–1866* (London, 1988) pp. 166–7.

(h) *English view of Austrian terms to Piedmont*

I do not attempt to point out any particular article of this
65 project for your observation; for there is not one in the whole treaty that is not objectionable, or which is not conceived for the purpose of humiliating this Country, and of reducing it to a state of vassalage to Austria ...

You will find ample proof in the Austrian Project of the
70 intention to exercise an undue influence in the internal affairs of Sardinia, and so to cripple the Sovereign and his Government as to render them for the future powerless. By this project the King is called upon to abrogate Laws passed by the Parliament by simple Royal Decree, and were he to
75 comply with the demands of Austria he would at the very commencement of his Reign have violated the Constitution he had just sworn to maintain. In short the terms now offered by Austria can only be described as an ungenerous attempt to crush a young Sovereign when in a moment of distress ...

Dispatch from Abercromby, British Minister at Turin, to Palmerston, 16 April 1849, in D. Beales, *The Risorgimento and the Unification of Italy* (London, 1981) pp. 152, 154.

Questions

★ a Was Charles Albert's promise to continue the struggle confirmed by subsequent events?

★ b Who was the Austrian Marshal in extract (f)? Verona formed part of what Austrian defensive unit?

c How does extract (f) differ from extract (e) in explaining the Piedmontese defeat?

d What does extract (g) suggest about Austria's treatment of Victor Emmanuel? Account for this.

e Explain the different versions of the Austrian terms in extracts (g) and (h).

---

3 The republicans fight on

(a) *Manin jettisons his earlier political caution*

In March, when I proclaimed the Venetian republic, I declared that territorial and political questions had to be definitely decided by the whole nation according to the general interests of Italy. In July, when I was forced to give way to the party
5 propagating lamentable fusionist propaganda, I said that everything that was being done was provisional and that the Italian Diet at Rome would make the final decisions. My opinions of March and July have not changed. From this you will see to what extent we are in substantial agreement.
10 But I cannot agree with you when you say that the recommencement of the war must be deferred till the constituent assembly nominates a central power to direct it. No central power can be elected in a short enough time to meet our war needs. I firmly believe that our cause will be lost if we do not
15 make use of what has happened in Vienna, and if we let popular enthusiasm languish …
You could well send your Tuscan militias into the Veneto, commanded by the brave General Garibaldi; and you could also encourage the population of the Papal States to cross the Po to
20 aid us, whether their government wants it or not. Our experience of the war of the princes has been all too painful. Now it is time for an awe-inspiring and formidable war of the people.
We must do what we can for each other. Long live Italy.

Manin to new head of Tuscan government, 30 October 1848, in P. Ginsborg, *Daniele Manin and the Venetian Revolution of 1848–49* (Cambridge, 1979) p. 320.

(b) *Rome takes the decisive step*

4 October 1848

25 The bitterest and also the most skilful adversary of the Jesuits, the famous abbe Vincenzo Gioberti, not content with the complete victory he won over that Congregation in getting it expelled from every State in Italy, even from Rome, has sought to enlarge his role and to raise himself to the level of a states-
30 man, opening new destinies to the Peninsula.

Another Italian, the lawyer Mazzini, equally able and more energetic than the abbe Gioberti, has set himself up with the same intention ... and put himself at the head of the unitary republican party, while Gioberti ... has declared himself the
35 head of the party of constitutional monarchy ...

16 November 1848

Blood has been shed, and that blood was Count Rossi's ... who died yesterday about one o'clock from the well-aimed blow ... of an assassin... . The assassin, protected by his com-
40 panions and the indifference of the people, was able quietly to escape!!

Order had only one energetic and highly intelligent repre-sentative ... left at Rome. This representative was Monsieur Rossi, and that is exactly why he was killed ...
45 *25 November 1858*

I have just learned ... that the Pope left the Quirnal Palace during the night.

> Dispatches of Belgian envoy in Rome, in D. Beales, *The Risorgimento and the Unification of Italy* (London, 1981) pp. 143–4.

(c) *The Republic declared*

Article 1 Papacy has fallen, *de facto* and *de jure*, from the tem-poral throne of the Roman State.
50 *Article 2* The Roman Pontiff shall enjoy all the guarantees necessary for the exercise of his spiritual power.

Article 3 The Government of the Roman State is to be a pure democracy, and to assume the glorious name of the Roman Republic.
55 *Article 4* The Roman Republic shall maintain with the rest of Italy relations required by a common nationality.

> Decree by Roman constituent assembly, 8 February 1849, in F. Eyck (ed.), *The Revolutions of 1848–49* (Edinburgh, 1972) p. 137.

(d) Social reform

Whereas it is the office and duty of a well-organised Republic to provide for the gradual amelioration of the condition of the most necessitous classes:

60 Whereas the improvement most urgent at the present moment is that of withdrawing as many families as possible from the evils resulting from crowded and unhealthy habitations ... the Constituent Assembly, at the suggestion of the Triumvirs, decrees:

65 1. The edifice hitherto used as the Holy Office, is henceforth dedicated to the use of necessitous families or individuals, who shall be allowed to have lodgings therein on payment of a small monthly rent ...

2. A large portion of the rural domains belonging to reli-
70 gious corporations ... shall be immediately divided into a given number of portions, sufficient for the maintenance of one or more necessitous families having no other means of subsistence.

Decrees issued by the Roman Republic, April 1849, in F. Eyck (ed.), *The Revolutions of 1848–49* (Edinburgh, 1972) pp. 138–9.

(e) Foreign impressions

[After the news of the Milanese rising of March 1848 reaches
75 Rome] The English – or at least those of the illiberal, bristling nature – too often met here, which casts out its porcupine quills against everything like enthusiasm ... laughed at all this. They have said that this people would not fight; when the Sicilians, men and women, did so nobly they said. 'Oh!
80 The Sicilians are quite unlike the Italians; you will see when the struggle come on in Lombardy, they cannot resist the Austrian forces a moment.' I said, 'That force is only physical; do not you think a sentiment can sustain them?' They reply, 'All stuff and poetry; it will fade the moment their blood
85 flows.' ... [After the Roman Republic was proclaimed in February 1849] I met some English; all their comfort was, 'It would not last a month' – 'They hoped to see these fellows shot yet' ... Mr Carlyle would be delighted with his countrymen. They are entirely ready and anxious to see a Cromwell
90 for Italy. They, too, think it is no matter what happens 'in the back parlor' when the people starve. What signifies that, if there is 'order' in the front? How dare they make a noise to disturb us yawning at billiards! I met an American. He 'had no confidence in the Republic.' Why? Because he 'had no
95 confidence in the People.' Why? Because 'they were not like *our* People.' Ah! Jonathan and John – excuse me, but I must say

the Italian has a decided advantage over you in the power of quickly feeling generous sympathy ...

> Margaret Fuller, radical American journalist, March 1848, February 1849, in L. J. Reynolds and S. B. Smith (eds), *These Sad But Glorious Days* (Yale, 1991) pp. 213, 256–7.

Questions

★ *a* What had been happening in Vienna in October 1848 to excite Manin?

  b Explain Manin's reference to 'war of the princes' (line 21).

  c In extract (a) is Manin's reading of his earlier statements reliable (lines 1–9)? (Compare with section 2 above.)

  d How do Gioberti's and Mazzini's aims differ as reported in extract (b)?

  e What does 'the temporal throne' mean in extract (c)? What does Article 4 suggest?

★ *f* What was the role of the Triumvirs? Who was their leading figure? What would the reaction to their decrees be from conservatives, socialists, papalists and liberals respectively?

---

4 Rome under seige

(a) *Mazzini rouses the citizens*

Brothers! to arms! Foreigners, enemies of the Roman people, are advancing. Republican Europe is watching you; their eyes are on you, these Poles, these Germans, and these Frenchmen, unfortunate apostles of Liberty, but not without glory in their misfortune;
5 Lombards, Genoese, Sicilians and Venetians are watching you.

> Triumvirs appeal to the Romans, April 1849, in J. Ridley, *Garibaldi* (London, 1974) p. 274.

(b) The Times's *version of events*

The Times was not happy about the French action, but their suspicion of France was not as strong as their fears of Red Republicanism. When Oudinot, instead of marching straight into Rome, was driven back on 30 April, *The Times* commented
10 that 'no one, certainly, anticipated that this modern invasion would find an Horatius Cocles on the bridge', and sent a special correspondent to Oudinot's headquarters, though they had no reporter in Rome. The reports of their correspondent with Oudinot were written entirely from the French point of view.

15 On 27 June he wrote that though he strongly disapproved of
Oudinot's expedition, he nevertheless hoped that the French
would capture Rome, because 'nothing will contribute so much
to the general peace of the world as the capture of that band of
Socialists who, under the name of liberty and by force of arms,
20 have held possession so long of the Eternal City'.

     J. Ridley, *Garibaldi* (London, 1974) p. 298.

(c) *An English resident's view*

28th June 1849 … The Moniteur this morning states the
number of *foreigners* in the Roman service to be 1,650: 800
Lombards; 300 Tuscans; 250 Poles and French; and 300 miscel-
laneous in Garibaldi's corps. The Natl Guard is 14,000 strong;
25 the Army, I suppose, 20,000. A bomb I am thankful to say has
left its mark on the façade of the Gesu. I wish it had stirred up
old Ignatius. 4 July 1849… . If you should happen to read in
the Constitionel ·that '*on Tuesday, July 3rd our army enterd
Rome amidst the acclamations of the people*' perhaps you will not
30 be the worse for a commentary on the text… . [The French
troops] looked a little awkward, while the people screamed and
hooted and cried Viva la Republica Romana etc… . A priest
who walked and talked publicly in the Piazza Colonna with a
Frenchman was undoubtedly killed. I know his friends and saw
35 one of them last night. Poor man, he was quite a liberal eccle-
siastic, they tell me: but certainly not a prudent one.

     F. L. Mulhauser (ed.), *The Correspondence of Arthur Hugh*
Clough (Oxford, 1957) I, pp. 264–5.

Questions

★ *a* In extract (a) explain Mazzini's reference to 'unfortunate
apostles of liberty' (lines 3–4) and his selection of Italians
(line 5).

★ *b* List the forces advancing on Rome.

  c In extract (b) who was this modern Horatius Cocles
(line 11)?

★ *d* Why should *The Times* have been so hostile to
the Roman Republic? Why were its reports inevitably
one sided?

★ *e* Why should Clough emphasise the word *foreigners*?
What are the Moniteur and the Constitionel? Who was
'old Ignatius'?

★ *f* Why should Clough and some other Englishmen have
supported the Roman Republic?

5 Reasons for failure

(a) Separatism

27 November 1850 I had a long conversation with M. Buonarotti, the representative of the great artist, formerly a judge, and now Councillor of State. He spoke with great but, perhaps, not undue bitterness of the republican faction, which, by the assassination of
5 Rossi, the Neapolitan revolt, the unjust attack on Austria, and the insurrections of Genoa, Leghorn, and Florence, has ruined the happiness of this generation, and thrown back Italy for a century. 'This little Duchy [Tuscany],' he said, 'is a specimen of Italian unity. Florence, Lucca, Siena, and Pisa all hate one
10 another, even more than they hate Austria.' Among the mischiefs which he feared from republicanism was trial by jury.
28 November First came the Duke Serra di Falco [a Sicilian refugee in Florence]. 'I regret Sicily', he said, 'but yet I amuse myself here.... Politics, on a great scale, were forced on me, and
15 I don't think that I shall ever take them up again. Men, at least my countrymen, are not worth the sacrifices which the attempt to serve them costs, and the attempt scarcely ever succeeds. Those who know what is right are too timid or too indolent to act on their convictions, and almost all the bold and active are
20 ignorant and perverse. When the whole united force of all Italy was not more than was wanted to drive out the Austrians, we wasted our strength in civil war, and never were more thoroughly disunited, never feared and hated one another more deeply, than when we were proclaiming Italy united.'
25 *5 December* ... I asked the Duke [Serra di Falco] if he agreed in Prince Butera's opinion that under no circumstances whatever, however liberal the Constitution, or however honest and intelligent the King, could Sicily and Naples live together comfortably under one sovereign. He answered. 'Perfectly; it is
30 lamentable, but it is true'.

> N. W. Senior, journals, in D. Mack Smith, *The Making of Italy, 1796–1866* (London, 1988) p. 165.

(b) Class

[After the Piedmontese defeat in August 1848] the republican party at Milan could have taken up the struggle if only it had been still in existence. Individual republicans had done nothing to indoctrinate the people, partly because they despaired of
35 success.... When the driving force and the overriding principle failed, the people were left leaderless. Their first and only aim, that of expelling all foreigners, remained unchanged. But where a regular army had lost, how could the ordinary people expect to win? Material interest might have urged them to continue

40 fighting without leaders, for only by experience could they have
become convinced of their own strength. But what was their real
interest? Whether ruled by a King, a President or a Triumvirate,
the people's slavery does not cease unless the social system can be
changed ...

45 The peoples of Rome and Venice were then left to struggle on
alone; but, like their governments, they were not informed by
any great integrating idea. In Rome it was thought that one
could save Italy by respecting old institutions, and people
marched to war under the banner of privilege and Catholicism.
50 Venice sought to take refuge from the shipwreck by isolating
herself. All Rome and Venice could do was save Italian honour.

> Carlo Pisacane, 1850–51, in D. Mack Smith, *The
> Making of Italy, 1796–1866* (London, 1988) pp. 158–60.

(c) *Rogues and trimmers*

[The suggestion that revolutionary governments should be nominated by those who led the initial insurrection] is not apt, at least
by our experience at Palermo. Does [that writer] know who led
55 the January 12 rising? It is something not to be set down in a
history book, but we must not conceal the fact from you and
other members of the National Committee. Those leaders were
Santoro, later killed by the people as a traitor; Miloro, who was
then arrested and tried in Sicily for misappropriation of public
60 funds, and who recently was implicated in another robbery in
Malta; Bivona, who now has a job as a forest guard under the
Bourbon ruler of Sicily; the Pagano brothers, who have now
become policemen and are cousins of the famous Malvica who
was given command of the police when the royalist counterrevo-
65 lution triumphed in Palermo; Scordato, who is also a police chief
in Bourbon Sicily; and Miceli, who has a job there as a customs
officer.

> La Farina to Mazzini, 1851, in D. Mack Smith, *The
> Making of Italy, 1796–1866* (London, 1988) pp. 135–6.

(d) *An indifferent countryside*

As Della Peruta has written, Mazzini had 'no deep awareness of
the stratified world of rural Italy, of the peasants without land, the
70 tenants and sharecroppers suffocating under the burden of exor-
bitant and semi-feudal contracts, the day labourers reduced to
absolute misery'. The lack of any specific social content in
Mazzini's political thinking, his inability to tackle the fundamen-
tal questions of agrarian reform, meant that although the
75 Lombardo–Venetian peasantry might have understood the kind of
war he wanted them to wage, they simply had no good reason to
wage it. In the towns, where newspaper propaganda was far more

extensive, where municipal pride transcended class barriers, nationalism was not the exclusive preserve of the middle classes.
80 But in the countryside, with so large a degree of isolation, illiteracy and suspicion, Mazzini's vague imprecations to revolt 'in the name of God and the people' fell upon deaf ears.

P. Ginsborg, *Daniele Manin and the Venetian Revolution of 1848–49* (Cambridge, 1979) p. 259.

(e) International hostility

On England no dependence can be placed. She is guided by no great idea; her Parliamentary leaders sneer at sentimental policy,
85 and the 'jargon' of ideas ... . Then the Church of England, so long an enemy to the Church of Rome, feels a decided interest with it on the subject of temporal possessions. The rich English traveler, fearing to see the Prince Borghese stripped of one of his palaces for a hospital or some such low use ... muses: 'I hope to
90 see them all shot yet, these rascally republicans.' How I wish my own country would show some noble sympathy when a experience so like her own is going on ... . [After the rebellions were suppressed] Order reigns – the same Order that reigned at Warsaw. Russian–Austrian clemency is yielded to those who
95 remain to share it ... The French have not redeemed one pretext by which they painted over the ugly face of their perfidy ... That [foreign] intervention, the falsehood of France, the inertia of England, the entrance of Russia into Hungary – all these steps tracked in blood, which cause so much anguish at the moment,
100 Democracy ought in fact to bless. They insure her triumphs – there is no possible compromise between her and the Old ... All the more for what has happened in these sad days, will entire Europe, at the end of this century, be under Republican form of Government.

Margaret Fuller, February, August 1849, in L. J. Reynolds and S. B. Smith (eds), *These Sad But Glorious Days* (Yale, 1991) pp. 259, 312–13.

Questions

a To what extent did M. Buonarotti and the Duke Serra di Falco agree about the reasons for the failures of 1848–9? Were they different in sympathy towards the Risorgimento?

b In extract (b) which states were ruled by a King, President or Triumvirate (line 42) in the risings of 1848–9?

c What can you tell about Pisacane's political viewpoint? Do the Roman Republic's decrees (section 3, extract (d)) confirm his strictures?

d In extract (c) explain the phrase 'it is not something to be set down in a history book'.

e Which of the other extracts does question d tend to confirm?

★ f Which of the reasons for failure, including factors not mentioned in these extracts, seem the most convincing for 1848–9?

IV Piedmont in the 1850s

Introduction

In the 1850s Piedmont was the only state to retain its constitution from the heady days of 1848. Whether this was because of, or despite, the King is open to question. The constitution enabled a parliamentary system to operate and a certain amount of civil liberties. From 1852 the chief minister was an aristocrat, Count Cavour, who achieved power by the *connubio*, or alliance, between the Left and liberal Centre forces in the assembly.

Cavour's aim simply was to modernise Piedmont. He reorganised the administration, introducing professional standards for many government departments. On the economic front he promoted railways – believed by liberals to be the engine for Italian unity – and did what he could to bring about free trade. He was unable to avoid taking on the Church and after deep opposition from the King and conservative factions, carried a Bill, which in summary – limiting the number of priests and appropriating revenues – sounds more draconic than it was in reality.

As will be seen in the next chapter, Cavour constantly pushed for 'Italian' interests on the international stage. Combined with his domestic reforms, this policy encouraged some nationalists to drop their insistence on a republican status for independent Italy. Mazzini, of course, could not compromise, but found his beliefs and tactics increasingly criticised.

1 Modernising Piedmont

(a) *Cavour achieves power*

You will remember the bases of the *connubio* – the fusion of the two Centre groups in the Piedmontese parliament – were laid down at your house in October 1851 and January 1852.... At that meeting we agreed to lay the foundations in
5 the Chamber for this fusion. Once this had been achieved, we would use the opportunity provided by some important parlimentary question to make it public. As a result, the *con-*

nubio declared its existence during the debate on a change in our press laws. Before this, however, the whole plan had already been agreed by these four men [Cavour, Rattazzi, Castelli, Buffa].

Two main principles were to inspire the new party. In home affairs we would resist all reactionary tendencies that might threaten after the recent *coup d'état* in France. At the same time, in so far as circumstances permitted, we would promote a continuous and progressive development of the freedoms allowed by our constitution, alike in politics, economics and administration. As regards international affairs, we would prepare the way for Piedmont to liberate Italy from foreign rule.

> U. Rattazzi to M. Castelli, 1 May 1870, in D. Mack Smith, *The Making of Italy, 1796–1866* (London, 1988) p. 176.

(b) *Victor Emmanuel and the constitution*

King Victor Emmanuel is in no sense liberal: his tastes, his education and his whole habit of behaviour all go the other way. He tells everyone that 'my father bestowed institutions on the country which are quite unfitted to its needs and the temper of its inhabitants'. To some people he will add, 'but my father and myself have both given our word, and I will not break it.' To others, however, he will say confidentially, 'I am only waiting for the *right moment to change everything*. The moment will be the outbreak of war. Whenever it comes, I shall be ready.' Any French official who finds himself alone with the King will be asked if the time has yet arrived ...

Victor Emmanuel, I repeat, does not like the existing constitution, nor does he like parliamentary liberties, nor a free press. He just accepts them temporarily as a kind of weapon of war. He keeps the tricolor flag instead of restoring that of Savoy; but he looks on it not as a revolutionary standard, only as a banner of conquest. Once the conquest is over, he will bring back the old flag; but at once on the outbreak of hostilities he would suspend the constitution indefinitely. One must therefore be not deceived by any talk about the chivalrous attitude of the King and his ministers to the constitution they have sworn to observe.

> French ambassador to French Foreign Minister, 16 October 1852, in D. Mack Smith, *The Making of Italy, 1796–1866* (London, 1988) pp. 170–1.

(c) *The Church's power and wealth curtailed*

The first clause [of a Bill put before the Piedmontese parlia-
ment] read: 'All the religious orders are declared abolished,
with the exception of the Sisters of Charity and those of St.
Joseph, and those Orders and Communities dedicated to public
5 instruction, preaching, of the care of the sick, which are mentioned by name in the list, approved by Royal decree, and published simultaneously with the present law.'

E. E. Y. Hales, *Pio Nono* (London, 1956) p. 179.

(d) *Cavour argues in favour*

Gentlemen, the various speakers who have risen to oppose this
Bill, using more or less excited language and carrying into the
10 discussion an unusual warmth, not to say passion, have condemned it as contrary to religion and the rights of property; as
leading to the application of fatal socialistic and communistic
doctrines; as violating formally sanctioned pacts; and finally as
odious, revolutionary and ruinous... .

15 It has been stated by certain speakers that, as a necessary and
inevitable consequence of this law, a great upheaval in the
country must ensue. This has been used by some as a warning,
by others as a threat. To these I will reply by the lessons of
history.

20 I will begin by declaring that I have too much trust in the
sense and patriotism of the episcopate and the national clergy
to believe that this danger could be realised. But if it should
happen, if this agitation should unhappily exceed a certain

limit, I would remind the Senate that it would not be the first
time that fatal struggles have taken place between the principles
of liberty and progress and that of reaction, cloaked beneath
the mantle of religion. In the seventeenth century in England
the reactionary party, led by the Jesuits, commenced a bitter
war on liberty and progress, and the result of that struggle was
the fearful catastrophe that dragged to irreparable ruin the old
and venerated line of the Stuarts. In times nearer to us in
France, after the restoration, a monarch not less enlightened
than prudent succeeded in re-establishing peace and harmony
between the new times and the old; but when to this monarch
another succeeded, who, having surrendered himself to a party
that, under the pretext of favouring religious interests, fought
all progress and liberty, another struggle broke out that resulted
in the ruin of the old throne of the Bourbons. I trust, gentlemen, that made wise by the lessons of history, such events will
not take place amongst us, nor do I believe that our venerable
clergy desire to imitate the examples I have brought before
you.

Cavour in the Senate, 25 April 1855, in A. J. Whyte, *The Political Life and Letters of Cavour* (Oxford, 1930) pp. 176–8.

(e) *D'Azeglio appeals to the King*

Your Majesty,
  In Spain it was forbidden to touch the King under pain of
death. There was one whose clothes caught fire; no one dared
to touch him and he was burned to death. But I, if I was to
risk my head, or even to lose utterly your favour, would consider myself the most vile of men if at a moment such as this I
did not write to you, since I have not been permitted to speak
to you in person.
  Your Majesty, believe an old and faithful servant, who in
serving you never had a thought but for your welfare, your
good name and the country's good; I say to you with tears in
my eyes and kneeling at your feet, *go no further on the road you
have taken*. There is still time. Retake the former one. An
intrigue of monks has in a day succeeded in destroying the
work of your reign; in agitating the country; imperilling the
Statute; besmirching your name for loyalty. There is not a
moment to lose. The official declarations in the last appeal
have not solved the question. It is said that the Crown seeks
new lights. Let the Crown say that these lights have shown the
proposed conditions to be unacceptable. Let them be considered as if they had not been, and things will retake their
normal and constitutional course as before. Piedmont will bear

65 anything; but, to be put again beneath the priestly yoke, no, per Dio!

> M. D'Azeglio to Victor Emmanuel, May 1855, in A. J. Whyte, *The Political Life and Letters of Cavour* (Oxford, 1930) p. 180.

Questions

   a Why were certain exceptions made in extract (c)?

★ *b* In extract (d) what seventeenth-century episode is being referred to? Why do you think Cavour explicitly mentions the Jesuits? Who was the French monarch (line 34)? What lesson does Cavour seek to teach from these historical examples?

   c In extract (d) explain 'episcopate' (line 21).

★ *d* How had D'Azeglio been a servant to the King?

   e What is the difference in style between extracts (c) and (d)?

   f In extract (e) what is the Statute (line 58)?

   g What do extracts (b) and (e) tell you about the King's attitude to these changes in Piedmont?

---

2 Republicans warm towards Piedmont

(a) *Manin's opinion*

I am sending you herewith the original and a translation of my declaration which has already been published in the *Times* and is coming out tomorrow in the *Siècle*.

Our republican party, so bitterly criticised, thus makes one
5 more act of abnegation and sacrifice in the national cause.

'Convinced that above all Italy must be made, that this is the first and most important question, we say to the Monarchy of Savoy: 'Make Italy and we are with you. – If not, not.'

And to the constitutionalists we say: 'Think about making
10 Italy and not of enlarging Piedmont; be Italians and not municipalists, and we are with you. – If not, not.'

I think it is time to give up existing party divisions based on purely secondary differences; the principal, vital matter is whether we are of the unifying nationalist school of thought,
15 or whether we belong to the separatist, municipalist school.

I, a republican, raise the banner of unity. If all those who want Italy gather round and defend it, then *Italy will be.*

> D. Manin to L. Valerio, 19 September 1855, in R. L. H. Lloyd, *Cavour and Italian Unification* (London, 1975) p. 15.

(b) *Differing views*

Foresti writes again to me as follows:

'Our Garibaldi went to Turin on the thirteenth and I went
20 with him. Cavour welcomed him with courtesy and friendli-
ness and hinted that he could rely on considerable official help.
Cavour even authorised Garibaldi to pass on these hints to
others. It seems that he is seriously thinking about the great
political redemption of our peninsula. Garibaldi took his leave
25 of the minister on very friendly terms and with these encouraging promises of help for the cause.'

It was all an act! What Cavour wants, *and I am sure of it*, is
just for Piedmont to be enlarged by a few square miles of
Italian soil.

> G. Pallavincino to D. Manin, 24 August 1856, in D.
> Mack Smith, *The Making of Italy, 1796–1866* (London,
> 1988) p. 216.

(c) *Dropping the purist line*

30 This is my reply to Mazzini ...

'Our view is that the 100,000 men in the Piedmontese
army are indispensable for any war of independence. We
want to entice, or if need be force, the King to act alongside
us. We will entice him by offering him the crown of Italy; or
35 we could force him by the threat of a republican revolution
which would deprive him of the crown of Piedmont-
Sardinia.

You on the other hand propose not committing ourselves on
the monarchy but remaining neutral on this issue. We
40 absolutely disagree with you here – not out of love for the
King, but because we distrust him. We do not want him to
abandon us halfway through; we do not want the dynasty to
exploit the revolution in order to fight Austria, and then use
diplomacy to fight against the revolution. We want to *compro-
45 mise the King* by dragging him into a revolutionary war; and we
shall do this by proving to him that the war will help the
dynasty and that it is necessary, indeed *inevitable*... .

Dear friend, show yourself a real hero. Sacrifice your cher-
ished republican views on the altar of the fatherland. Another
50 great republican, Daniele Manin, has shown you the way.

It is not enough to say '*unification!*' The idea is too vague. If
unification is to be understood by the masses, it must be trans-
lated into something more solid and more personal. Our
formula '*Vittorio Emanuele King of Italy*', is therefore a necessity.
55 Either we adopt it, or there will be no rising; though of course
we can change our programme if tomorrow the conditions of
Europe change.'

G. Pallavincino to D. Manin, 4 September 1856, in D. Mack Smith, *The Making of Italy, 1796–1866* (London, 1988) p. 217.

(d) *Living with the House of Savoy*

Here then is the noble purpose of the National Society. We want to unify Italy, so that all the powerful elements which she
60 embraces may cooperate in her liberation. We want harmony between the ideas which prepared revolution and the facts which enact them, between the pen and the sword, intelligence and force: harmony between province and province, city and city, class and class within the nation. We do not rebuff the
65 aristocracy which agrees to recognize the needs of our civilization, and we embrace the democracy which agrees to keep itself within the limits of justice and equity ... Finally, harmony between the house of Savoy and Italy, so that the house of Savoy may know how to hold the standard of Italian
70 independence high, respected and glorious! No element of strength is rejected by the *Italian National Society*, which leaves full liberty of opinion and action to its members ... so long as they do not refuse the cooperation of the house of Savoy in the great task of the emancipation of the patria ... We are not so
75 childish to be frightened by the name of king, for we know well from our experiences that liberty can be enjoyed under a civil principate, as servitude can be endured under a republican regime.

G. La Farina, Political Credo of the National Society, 1858, in S. J. Woolf, *The Italian Risorgimento* (New York, 1969) p. 62.

(e) *Mazzini reprimanded by his followers*

We must tell you, privately but clearly, that your sources of
80 information about public opinion are wrong. Honest they may be, but they have deceived you into thinking the whole of Italy a volcano ready to erupt, as though the courage of the revolutionaries would be enough to galvanise the country, as though a handful of unarmed men could destroy a foreign domination
85 which has lasted for centuries. You are too credulous; you think the people are behind you, whereas unfortunately they are not nearly so restless and are certainly not permanently waiting to start a revolution. The ordinary people are neither educated enough, nor have they the strength to move or to
90 support a revolution once it has begun; they require the immediate support of that other large social class on whom they depend for guidance, for encouragement, and even for their daily bread.

These are your mistakes, the fatal delusions which have led
95 you from error into error, and so have caused you to forfeit the
allegiance of most of our republicans who still retain the ability
to think for themselves. Many of your old adherents have
become so discouraged that they have turned to other parties
and policies ...
100 Your mistakes, and they are serious, are these: to impose
action at a moment chosen by yourself, even without prepara-
tion and with too few people, to think that a simple insurrection can be converted quickly into an extensive revolution ...

A. Bertani and others to Mazzini, January 1858, in
D. Mack Smith, *The Making of Italy, 1796–1866*
(London, 1988) p. 222.

Questions

a What did Manin mean by 'one more act of abnegation
and sacrifice'? What is the importance of this change?

b Why should Cavour's friendly reception of Garibaldi
cause surprise? Why did Pallavicino distrust these
overtures? Why should Cavour only hint at official help?

c Account for the apparent changes towards Piedmont by
Pallavicino in extracts (b) and (c).

d How is Mazzini advised to change his line in extract (c)?
What is meant by a revolutionary war (line 45)?

e In extract (e) explain 'that other large social class' (line 91).

★ f Give examples of Mazzini's 'mistakes' (line 94) in the
1850s.

V   The International Stage

Introduction

One of the lessons of 1848/9 had been that Piedmont could not hope to defeat Austria without foreign aid. The Crimean War seemed to present a chance to extract a bargain for Piedmontese support. It was not quite that simple, however. Austria was the obvious candidate as ally for the hard-pressed western powers, thus placing Piedmont in the difficult position of fighting alongside its clear enemy. There was also no question of either England or France promising an alliance against Austria after the war; the most the Piedmontese could hope for was a seat at the subsequent peace conference, with the aim of raising the 'Italian question', and perhaps the morsel of a north Italian duchy.

It has long been assumed that Cavour was singlehandedly responsible for Piedmont's entry into the war, but there is evidence that the King was the driving force over this issue. Unfortunately peace occurred before the small Piedmontese force could make much of a mark. Cavour did attend the Congress of Paris and sent back enthusiastic (and perhaps wishful) reports of British and French encouragement. The final resolution, however, saw Piedmont with neither additional territory nor an alliance against Austrian power in Italy.

Peversely enough it was to take Orsini's assassination attempt to set Napoleon III on the path to helping Piedmont. Historians have disagreed over the manner and extent of the Emperor's aid. The form of the new Italy envisaged by Cavour and Napoleon at Plombières and the subsequent treaty needs to be carefully distinguished. Their aims were not identical, although both feared the more uncompromising Italian nationalism and any hint of social revolution.

Once the treaty had been signed, the task for Cavour was to provoke Austria into aggressive action before Napoleon's resolution faltered or Europe moved collectively against war.

1 Piedmont enters the Crimean War

(a) Diplomatic difficulties

I perceived from your letter of the thirteenth [which also offered English support against Austria if the latter 'interfered' with Piedmont] that your Lordship considers Austria will eventually enter entirely into the views and policies of England
5 and France – that is to say will join in the war against Russia. In that case you would naturally desire to have exact information as to the part which Italy could take when Austria is engaged with Russia. Will Italy rise in revolution against Austria, the Pope and the King of Naples? If so how is that
10 revolution to be mastered and suppressed?

So far as Piedmont is concerned I am convinced that she will act with good faith in any case. But she would be placed in a dilemma. She would feel that she could not draw the sword for Austria and against Italians. She would do nothing. She would be
15 neutral and neutralised; and of no use either to herself or the Western Powers; and a source of constant anxiety to Austria. An Italian revolution would tend to the advantage of Russia and in great measure palsy the action of Austria in your cause ...

[Hudson now paraphrases Cavour's opinion] Piedmontese
20 statesmen hold that the proper position of Austria is that of a barrier to Russia on the Danube and in the Black Sea. They say: – give Austria Bessarabia, the provinces of the Danube and the Crimea; make her the eastern bulwark of Europe. In exchange for the Danube and the Crimea, give Sardinia
25 Lombardy and Venice. This places 70,000 good and picked bayonets at the service of the common cause. Italy is tranquillised. The questions of Tuscany, Rome and Naples would insensibly, gradually, but surely be solved. The states would find their safety lie in granting such reforms as would disarm
30 the revolutionary spirits; and, if not, Piedmont with the additional five millions of Italians would be strong enough to crush any and every attempt at revolution: for her dynasty, her independence and her organisation are of old date, and her citizen, like her army, is accustomed to discipline and to obey.... .
35 It is too much to expect of Piedmont that she could follow England and France without hopes of extension to territory.

> Sir James Hudson, British minister at Turin, to Lord Clarendon, 24 October 1854, in D. Mack Smith, *The Making of Italy, 1796–1866* (London, 1988) pp. 192–4.

(b) Victor Emmanuel enthusiastic

The Duke [de Gramont, French ambassador to Piedmont]: Am I to understand that your Majesty wishes to join France in our

40   alliance with England and contribute your contingent of
troops?

The King: Yes, that is my wish, and it will be done. It was on
my orders that Cavour spoke of it, and if the ministers have
to be changed, I shall change them. But don't say anything
about it; leave me to act. Oh, they make me laugh with their
45   fears! But it's really the only sensible thing to do. Once our
soldiers are aligned alongside yours, I shan't care a fig for
Austria. Besides, one must do something. If we don't send
our soldiers to Russia, we shall be led instead by all these
noisy revolutionaries into committing a blunder of some sort
50   in Italy. One must be blind not to see it. Cavour is too much
taken up with his Lombard friends. Their turn will come
later. I want to help them too, but that mustn't hold us up.

> The French ambassador interviews Victor Emmanuel,
> June 1854, in D. Mack Smith, *The Making of Italy,
> 1796–1866* (London, 1988) p. 197.

(c) *Piedmont agrees to enter on certain conditions*

The Sardinian Government desires to adhere simultaneously
to the offensive and defensive treaty of April 10th between
55   the governments of France and England, at the same time it
will sign a convention by which it undertakes to furnish a
contingent of 15,000 men, on conditions to be fixed, and of
which the first is the loan of two millions sterling at 3 per
cent, payable after the war on conditions to be determined
60   hereafter.

The two Western Powers declare that they will, at the con-
clusion of peace, take into consideration the services rendered
to the coalition by the Sardinian Government and the sacrifices
made in men and money.

65   By the treaty the Sardinian Government enters the
European Concert; takes part in the negotiations, and sits at
the Congress held for the re-establishing of peace and restoring
the European equilibrium.

Secret Articles ... (2) The high contracting parties will upon
70   the re-establishment of peace take into consideration the state
of Italy.

> 14 December 1854, in A. J. Whyte, *The Political Life and
> Letters of Cavour* (Oxford, 1930) p. 138.

(d) *Cavour in favour of the treaty*

But how, I shall be asked, can this treaty ever help Italy? I
will reply: in the only way given to us, or perhaps to anyone,
to help Italy in the actual conditions of Europe. The experi-
75   ence of the past years and of the past centuries has demon-

strated – at least in my opinion – how little conspiracies, plots, revolutions and unorganised outbreaks have helped Italy. Far from helping her, they have been one of the greatest calamities that afflicted this beautiful part of Europe. And not only because of the great number of individual misfortunes, which came from them, but because these continuous conspiracies, these repeated revolutions, these ill-ordered movements, had the effect of lessening the esteem, and, up to a certain point, the sympathy, which the other peoples of Europe entertained for Italy.

Now I believe that the principal condition for improving the lot of Italy, the condition which overtops all the others, is to raise her reputation again, to act in such ways that all the peoples of the earth, rulers and subjects alike, shall render justice to her qualities, and for this, two things are necessary: first to prove to Europe that Italy has enough civilised judgement to govern herself in orderly fashion, to rule with liberty, that she is in condition to employ the most perfect forms of government known; second, that her military worth is equal to that of her ancestors.

Cavour in the assembly, 6 February 1855, in R. L. H. Lloyd, *Cavour and Italian Unification, 1854–60* (London, 1975) p. 12.

Questions

a   Why should Piedmont be placed in a dilemma by the allied invitation to join the war?

b   In extract (a) what was 'the common cause' (line 26)?

c   Why does Cavour in extract (a) believe there would be no revolution in Tuscany, Rome and Naples?

d   In extract (b) why should the King feel it might be necessary to change his ministers?

e   What blunder did he fear if the army stayed at home?

f   How did the agreement benefit the western powers and Piedmont respectively?

★ *g*   Britain and France refused to allow the secret articles. Why?

★ *h*   Which groups were responsible for those risings Cavour condemned in extract (d)? Why might 'Europe' have been unsympathetic?

i   Account for the difference between Piedmont's aims in extract (a) and the reality of extract (d).

2 At the Congress of Paris

(a) *Piedmontese aims*

This cessation of war is deplorable from our point of view. I regret it bitterly. But we must accept the inevitable and make all we can of the unfortunate position in which that artful old woman Austria has placed us.

5   In England, where the war was popular, we can make our discontent public and let our opinion about Austria be unreservedly voiced. In France we need to handle things more tactfully, so as not to shock the Emperor who sees this peace as the triumph of his policy ...

10   If we should succeed in getting our allies to admit the necessity of forcing Austria to withdraw her troops from the Romagna, we shall have achieved a good deal, for the destruction of the temporal powers of the papacy will have been admitted in principle. Judging by impressions during my visit

15 to England, this idea is pretty favourably reviewed by their government, especially by Lord Palmerston. He spoke about giving Tuscany the papal legations in the Romagna. At first I rejected this proposal, as I still would if the war had continued, but now we must clutch it as a straw. If the Pope's states were

20 to be divided between Tuscany and Modena, Piedmont would inevitably have to be compensated. I personally would be satisfied with the duchies of Piacenza, Massa and Carara. You can say all this quite openly. It will come much better from you than from a professional diplomat.

> Cavour to Lamarmora in the Crimea, 21 January 1856, in D. Mack Smith, *The Making of Italy, 1796–1866* (London, 1988) pp. 202–3.

(b) *France apparently sympathetic*

25 At my urging and with the strong solicitations of Lord Clarendon, the Emperor consented today to hold a sort of conference attended by Lord Clarendon, Count Walewski, and me... . The Emperor manifested the liveliest and most sincere desire to do something for Italy. He was quite aware

30 of the immense inconveniences which would result from the silences of the Congress on the affairs of the Peninsula. He recognised the sorry condition of the provinces governed by the Pope. In short he assented to my entire presentation. When we finally came to look for ways to take action,

35 Count Walewski raised all sorts of difficulties. He pointed out all the things Count Buol would do to avoid or distract this discussion. Lack of authority, absence of instructions, etc. The Emperor, a practical man, was very astonished by

the objections of his Minister. He was ready to propose the
40 revision of all the treaties of 1815.

After a discussion which lasted no less than two hours, in
which I took the most active role, thanks to the support of
Lord Clarendon, the Emperor ended up by giving a precise
order to Walewski to place before the Congress two questions,
45 that of Greece and that of the Roman States. This is a first
result achieved. It is not great, but nevertheless it cost me a
great deal.

> Cavour to Cibrario, 19 March 1856, in M. Walker,
> *Plombières* (New York, 1968) pp. 118–19.

Questions

a Why did Cavour regret the end of the war?
★ b Why were Austrian troops in the Romagna?
c Explain the last sentence in extract (a). What was
Lamarmora's profession?
★ d Identify Lord Clarendon and Counts Walewski and Buol.
★ e What were the treaties of 1815? Why might the French
be not averse to changing them?
f What does the tone of extract (b) tell you about Cavour's
character?

(c) *England apparently sympathetic*

I have just seen Clarendon. Here is a résumé of our talk. I said:
'You see, My Lord, that two things now follow: (1) Austria has
decided to make no concessions at all. (2) Italy has nothing left
to hope for from diplomacy. As a result, Piedmont's position is
5 very difficult. Either we must make a rapprochement with
Austria and the Pope, in which case I must resign in favour of
the reactionaires; or else we must, prudently of course, prepare
to fight Austria, in which case I must know if this would go
against the views of our best ally, England.'
10 Clarendon stroked his chin furiously, but did not seem
astonished. After a moment's silence he replied: 'You are quite
right. There is nothing else you can do. Only one must not say
so openly.'
I then added: 'You have been able to see here that I am
15 prudent and can keep my own counsel. I know that we will
have to await an opportune moment, but in the meantime we
must know what we are aiming at. War does not frighten me.
We are determined to fight *à l'outrance, to the knife*. But, for the
short time that the war lasted, you would have to help us.'

20   Here Clarendon left off playing with his chin and cried: '*Certainly, certainly*, and you could count on enthusiastic, energetic help.' My last word was, 'With Lamarmora we will give the Austrians something to think about.' 'Yes indeed,' he replied, 'I am sure of it.'

25   We then spoke of tomorrow's session, and he assured me that if Buol opened his mouth he would reply even more firmly than the other day. He encouraged me to go and see Queen Victoria. In sum, he seemed to look very favourably on our *third war of liberation*. You can say a few words of all this to
30 Palmerston, but taking care to keep it *a long way below* what I have said.

> Cavour to E. d'Azeglio, 11 April 1856, in D. Mack Smith, *The Making of Italy, 1796–1866* (London, 1988) pp. 204–5.

(d) *Clarendon's version*

Your Lordships have probably read some letters of the late Count Cavour which have recently been published in the newspapers... . It amounts to this, that I encouraged Count
35 Cavour to pick a quarrel with Austria – in fact, to declare war against her, by an assurance that in such a course of policy Piedmont would have the material support of England... . Out of the numerous conversations that I had with Count Cavour, the only one I can remember which could – I will not say
40 justify – but give rise to his assertion that I said 'If you are in a strait, we shall come to your assistance,' had reference, not to a war by Piedmont against Austria, but to an invasion of Piedmont by Austria, which was a fixed idea in Count Cavour's mind... . But that I, as one of Her Majesty's
45 Secretaries of State, without any communication from my colleagues, and contrary to the dictates of common sense, knowing that the French Emperor at that time had not the slightest thought or intention of making war against Austria,
50 that he did not then even require her to withdraw her troops from the Legations, until he had withdrawn his own troops from Rome – that I, under such circumstances, should, even in the most indirect manner, have recommended a country to which we heartily wished well to commit such a suicidal act as
55 going to war with Austria, with her large army under Radetzky, and having the support of Tuscany, Parma, Modena, and Naples – and that, without the shadow of authority for doing so, I should have given any pledge for the support of England in such a policy as would have imbroiled us in war
60 with half Europe – is an absurdity so palpable that I hope your Lordships will think it carries with it its own refutation,

without my laying claim to that character for extreme reserve and discretion for which Count Cavour rather paradoxically on that occasion informed his correspondent I was notorious.

> Lord Clarendon, House of Lords, 17 February 1862, in
> M. Walker, *Plombières* (New York, 1968) pp. 134–8.

(e) *Cavour sums up to the Piedmontese parliament*

65 What benefit then has Italy obtained from the Congress? We have gained two things, first, that the anomalous and unhappy condition of Italy has been proclaimed to Europe, not by demagogues, or revolutionaries, excited journalists, or party men, but by representatives of the greatest nations in Europe; by
70 statesmen at the head of their countries' Governments; by distinguished men accustomed to consult the dictates of reason rather than the impulse of emotion. That is the first fact, which I consider of the greatest value. The second is that these same powers have declared that, not only in the interests of
75 Italy herself, but in the interests of Europe, a remedy must be found for the evils from which Italy is suffering. I cannot believe that the sentiments expressed and the advice given by such nations as France and England can remain for long, sterile of results.

> Cavour to Chamber of Deputies, 6 May 1856, in
> A. J. Whyte, *The Political Life and Letters of Cavour*
> (Oxford, 1930) pp. 222–3.

Questions

   a In extract (c) explain the *third war of liberation* (line 29).

★ *b* Why were there French troops in Rome?

   c What significance is the distinction over an Austrian–Piedmontese war made by Clarendon in extract (d)?

   d Account for the discrepancies between Cavour's and Clarendon's discussion in extracts (c) and (d).

   e What do these documents reveal about Cavour's methods as a diplomat? What were his strengths and weaknesses?

★ *f* Name some of the demagogues, revolutionaries and journalists Cavour was thinking of in extract (e).

   g Considering all the documents in this section – extracts (a) to (e) – would you say Cavour was satisfied by the outcome of the Paris Congress?

---

3 Plombières

(a) *Austrian apprehensions of Napoleon*

There is no doubt that in these agitated days Napoleon's ideas
waver from one extreme to another, and the most contradictory decisions, or rather wishes to take decisions, follow each
other in his mind... . My despatch today runs as follows... . It
5   may be the trial of Orsini, and the letters of that assassin which
seemed to show up Napoleon as the arbiter of Italy's fate.
Moreover the continuous activity which the Italian national
party pursues here, with the idea of dragging Napoleon to the
point where he will intervene in the affairs of the peninsula,
10   this too has upset his thinking, for it has flattered the Emperor's
ego and reminded him of another period in his life which he
can never entirely forget.

> Diary of Count Hubner, Austrian ambassador in Paris,
> 9 April 1858, in D. Mack Smith, *The Making of Italy
> 1796–1866* (London, 1988) p. 233.

(b) *Cavour and Napoleon plan Italy's future*

As soon as I entered the Emperor's study, he raised the question
which was the purpose of my journey. He began by saying that
15   he had decided to support Piedmont with all his power in a
war against Austria, provided that the war was undertaken for a
nonrevolutionary end which could be justified in the eyes of
diplomatic circles – and still more in the eyes of French and
European public opinion.
20   Since the search for a plausible excuse presented our main
problem before we could agree, I felt obliged to treat that
question before any others... . The Emperor came to my aid,
and together we set ourselves to discussing each state in Italy,
seeking grounds for war. It was very hard to find any. After we
25   had gone over the whole peninsula without success, we arrived
at Massa and Carrara, and there we discovered what we had
been so ardently seeking ... we went on to the main question:
what would be the objective of the war?
        The Emperor readily agreed that it was necessary to drive
30   the Austrians out of Italy once and for all, and to leave them
without an inch of territory south of the Alps or west of the
Isonzo. But how was Italy to be organised after that? After a
long discussion, which I spare Your Majesty, we agreed more
or less to the following principles, recognizing that they were
35   subject to modification as the course of the war might determine. The valley of the Po, the Romagna, and the Legations
would form a kingdom of Upper Italy under the House of
Savoy. Rome and its immediate surroundings would be left to

the Pope. The rest of the Papal States, together with Tuscany,
40   would form a kingdom of central Italy. The Neapolitan frontier would be left unchanged. These four Italian states would
form a confederation on the pattern of the German Bund, the
presidency of which would be given to the Pope to console
him for losing the best part of his estates ...

45   After we had settled the fate of Italy, the Emperor asked me
what France would get, and whether Your Majesty would cede
Savoy and the County of Nice. I answered that Your Majesty
believed in the principle of nationalities and realized accordingly
that Savoy ought to be reunited with France; and that conse-
50   quently you were ready to make this sacrifice, even though it
would be extremely painful to renounce the country which had
been the cradle of your family and whose people had given your
ancestors so many proofs of affection and devotion. The question
of Nice was different, because the people of Nice, by origin, lan-
55   guages, and customs, were closer to Piedmont than France, and
consequently their incorporation into the Empire would be contrary to that very principle for which we were taking up arms.
The Emperor stroked his moustache several times, and merely
remarked that these were for him quite secondary questions
60   which we could discuss later ...

     Success will thus require very considerable forces. The
Emperor's estimate is at least 300,000 men, and I think he is
right ... France would provide 200,000 men. Piedmont and
the other Italian provinces 100,000 ...

65   The Emperor answered that he was very eager for the mar-
riage of his cousin with Princess Clotilde, since an alliance
with the House of Savoy was what he wanted more than anything else ... I tried not to offend him, yet I took pains to
make no commitment.

> Cavour to Victor Emmanuel, 24 July 1858, in
> D. Beales, *The Risorgimento and the Unification of Italy*
> (London, 1981) pp. 155–9.

(c) *The treaty*

70   *Article 1* If aggression by Austria leads to war between the
Piedmontese King and the Emperor of Austria, an offensive
and defensive alliance will come into force between the
Emperor of the French and the King of Piedmont–Sardinia.

     Article 2 The aims of the alliance will be to liberate Italy from
75   Austrian occupation, to satisfy the wishes of the people, and to
end the complications which threaten war and keep Europe
unsettled. The object would be, if the issue of the war so
permit, to create a Kingdom of Upper Italy with about eleven
million inhabitants.

80   *Article 3* The Duchy of Savoy and the Province of Nice will, by the same principle, be reunited to France.

    Article 4 Whatever happens in the war, it is expressly stipulated that the interests of the Catholic religion and the sovereignty of the Pope shall be maintained.

85   *Article 5* The cost of the war will be born by the Kingdom of Upper Italy.

    Article 6 The High Contracting Parties will accept no overtures for peace without previous agreement... .

    Military convention. Article 1 The allied forces in Italy shall rise
90   to about 300,000 men, of which 200,000 will be French and 100,000 Piedmontese... .

    Financial convention. Article 1 All the expenses of the war will be reimbursed to France by annual payments of one-tenth of all the revenues of the Kingdom of Upper Italy.

> Treaty between France and Piedmont, January 1859 (but antedated to 12 December 1858) in D. Mack Smith, *The Making of Italy, 1796–1866* (London, 1988) pp. 259–60.

Questions

★ *a* What reasons did Hubner offer for Napoleon's support for Italian nationalism? Explain 'another period in his life' (line 11).

   b In extract (b) what was considered essential to justify to public opinion the projected war against the Austrians? Explain war 'for a nonrevolutionary end' (line 17).

   c What grounds are there in extract (b) for accusing both Cavour and Napoleon III of cynical opportunism?

   d In the future Italy what was planned for Venetia?

   e What was the Pope's likely reaction to his role as president of this Italian confederation?

   f In extract (b) explain 'cradle of your family' (line 52).

   g Why should the Emperor have been keen to marry into the House of Savoy?

   h What is meant by 'the same principle' in Article 3?

   i How do Articles 2, 3 and 4 of the Treaty differ from the terms at Plombières? What are the other major differences? Which of the articles was least likely to be carried out by Piedmont?

4 The Road to War

(a) *Provoking Austria*

Cavour's draft for Victor Emmanuel's speech at the opening of the Piedmontese parliament was sent to Napoleon III for comment. The manuscript was returned with the last paragraph cancelled by the pencil of Napoleon, with the following
5   words in the margin, 'I find this too strong and I should prefer something like the following,' and then in the pen of Mocquard was a paragraph containing the words:

'If Piedmont, small though it is in territory, counts for something in the Councils of Europe, it is due to the greatness
10   of the ideals it represents and the sympathies it inspires. This position, without doubt, creates for us many dangers, yet, while we respect treaties, we cannot remain insensible to the *cris de douleur* that reach us from so many parts of Italy!' When Cavour read the Emperor's emendation, he was as puzzled as
15   he was pleased.

> 'I have received the Emperor's notes upon the speech [he writes to Nigra on 7 January 1859]. He finds the last paragraph too strong, and proposed by way of substitution, another, in which it is a question of "cris de douleur" rising
> 20   from all parts of Italy. But this is 100 times stronger! What the devil does he mean? Truly I don't yet know what we shall make of it. Tell the Prince [Jerome Napoleon] that this allusion to cries of grief will produce an immense effect.'

25   ... The effect was tremendous. Delivered firmly and clearly, with all that proud kingliness that marked Victor Emmanuel's public demeanour, it created an indelible impression. The applause was frantic and the exiles from all parts of Italy who crowded the galleries made no attempt to hide their emotion.

From A. J. Whyte, *The Political Life and Letters of Cavour* (Oxford, 1930) pp. 271–2.

(b) *Mazzini condemns Plombières*

... republicans by conviction believe ... that peoples cannot
30   redeem themselves or make of themselves nations through a lie, but only through principles, and earnest adoration of truth, and testimony bravely borne to conscious right; that the unity and liberty of an oppressed and dismembered people cannot be attained by the concessions or gifts of others, but must be con-
35   quered by the energetic efforts and sacrifices of the believers in that unity and liberty; that no nationality can be founded by foreign arms, but only by the battles of those who are called to compose and represent that nationality ... that the country of the Italians embraces the whole extent of territory between the

40 frontier of the Alps and the farthest shores of Sicily; that
national sovereignty consists in the free choice by the vote of
the people of the institutions which give form to the internal
life of the nation ... that any war wherein Italians should
combat in the name of independence, disjoined from that of
45 liberty, would lead to tremendous delusions, and the mere sub-
stitution of new masters for old; that any war in which the
Italians should delude themselves with the idea of conquering
liberty and independence under the auspices of, or through the
alliance of, Louis Napoleon Bonaparte, would be alike a folly
50 and a crime ... that between the combatants for an Italian
country and Louis Napoleon Bonaparte stands the indelible
eternal protest of the blood of Rome.

> Mazzini's public declaration, 28 February 1859, in
> D. Mack Smith, *The Making of Italy, 1796–1866*
> (London, 1988) pp. 263–4.

(c) *Napoleon III wavers*

This morning, without my asking for an audience, the
Emperor summoned me to the Tuileries for a talk. He began
55 by confessing that he was in the most difficult and dangerous
position conceivable. Certain indiscretions had been commit-
ted, some of them unavoidable, so that Europe now guessed
our plans; with the result that public opinion, especially in
England and Germany, has become scared of French ambition
60 and suddenly turned bitterly against him. He concludes that
we must temporarily suspend our plans... .

Public opinion here in France, as in Germany and England,
is against the war. In Paris, the middle classes, the Stock
Exchange, the Orleanists, officialdom, all are against it.

> Nigra to Cavour, 4 March 1859, in D. Mack Smith, *The
> Making of Italy, 1796–1866* (London, 1988) pp. 269–70.

(d) *The crisis reached*

65 *19 April* At my office I found despatches announcing that
France too [as well as England] is proposing disarmament and
admission of Piedmont to a general Congress together with all
the other Italian states. It is very grave news ... all Count
Cavour's colleagues blame him for having put too much faith
70 in N. III ... the Count leapt out of bed and told Ayme very
excitedly: 'The only thing left for me now is to blow out my
brains.' He immediately sent off a long telegram to Massimo
d'Azeglio saying that as France asks for disarmament, he must
submit. He spoke of resignation. He was annoyed, deeply
75 upset, and alone... . On my way to lunch I ran into Count
Cavour ... he said to me in an excited voice and with impul-

sive gestures: 'English policy has won. All is lost. N. III has abandoned us.'

21 April I received a note from West asking me to call on him
80 immediately ... it was a telegram from Lord Malmesbury dated 2 p.m. from London today. It said to tell Cavour that the Austrian ultimatum was sent from Vienna on Tuesday evening, in other words that Austria has entirely rejected the British propositions. The ultimatum has a three-day limit ... I accom-
85 panied West to the Ministry of the Interior where we found Cavour and Lamarmora. I entered in quite a frenzy to tell them about the despatch. The Count leapt up rubbing his hands more energetically than usual, and told me to bring West in at once. What a moment! It was a quarter to five. We all
90 remained standing. West read the despatch in a calm, slow voice; the Count asked him to read it over again, and when that had been done he said with great dignity: 'I hope you will agree that we have done everything in our power to avoid a conflagration.'

Massari's diary, in D. Mack Smith, *The Making of Italy, 1796–1866* (London, 1988) pp. 274–5.

Questions

a Why should Cavour have sent the draft of the King of Sardinia's speech to the Emperor of France?

b Are Mazzini's impressions concerning the agreement at Plombières factually accurate? Summarise his objections.

c Explain Mazzini's reference to 'the blood of Rome' (line 52).

★ d Why should England and Germany, and the French opinion distinguished by Nigra, have been against the war?

e Account for Napoleon III's apparent inconsistency in extracts (a), (c) and (d).

f In extract (d) why was Piedmont's admission to the Congress 'grave news' (line 68)?

★ g What did the Austrian ultimatum demand from Piedmont?

h In extract (d) how honest was Cavour's last remark (line 92)?

i What justification do these documents provide for the view that Cavour was more lucky than skilful in bringing the Plombières agreement into effect?

VI Chequered Advance in North and Centre

Introduction

The war in North Italy was shortlived. French forces defeated the Austrians at Magenta to enter Milan, in June 1859, and three weeks later, assisted by the Piedmontese army, won again at the battle of Solferino. It came as a surprise to some then, that next month Napoleon III alone should conclude an armistice with the Austrians at Villafranca, accepting Lombardy for Piedmont, but leaving Venetia within the Austrian Empire.

His reasons are open to argument, but one certain factor was the disconcerting development in central Italy. From April onwards there had been risings in the Romagna and Duchies, accompanied by calls to join with Piedmont. This had not been allowed for in the official treaty between Piedmont and France. Cavour naturally encouraged the process – though sometimes fearing the social consequences of popular unrest – but the French were dismayed to find themselves indirectly assisting at the birth of a much larger Italy than originally planned.

After Villafranca Cavour resigned in a fury. The quick pace of events in central Italy continued, however, despite Papal protests and French condemnation. It is important to be clear about the chronology here. In the autumn of 1859 the central states voted for annexation by Piedmont, then in October amalgamated to form Emilia under the leadership of the nationalist, Luigi Farini. Meanwhile Napoleon was gradually abandoning his opposing role, although final French acceptance to Piedmont's annexation of central Italy had to wait until France received the border provinces of Savoy and Nice. In the end Piedmont obtained more, and less, than had been intended at Plombières: much of central Italy, but no Venetia.

How much of this advance had been because of Cavour's skill and diplomacy; or was it simply the case of Piedmont waiting for the plums to fall into its lap? Were there conflicting aims among the nationalists in central Italy? Why was the Pope's position so weak? And, more importantly, what explained the torturous manoeuvrings of Napoleon III?

1 Risings in Tuscany

(a) *Cavour advises on tactics*

However little need there is for me to give you further information about the intentions of the King's Government, which
are well known, nevertheless I exhort you and *charge you to use
all your influence to prevent street demonstrations* and above all to
5 avoid a collision with the troops of the Grand Duke. The
former are almost always useless, and especially so now: in the
great enterprise for which Italy is preparing, it is desirable that
we shun the errors of 1848 and 1849, among which, and not
least, ought to be numbered the disorderly shouting of multi-
10 tudes. Once the push has been given, it is very difficult to hold
back the most enthusiastic.

> Cavour to Boncompagni, Piedmontese representatives in
> Florence, 20 March 1859, in D. Beales, *The Risorgimento
> and the Unification of Italy* (London, 1981) p. 165.

(b) *Duke Leopold flees*

Since the events of April 27th, a certain uneasiness weighs on
people's minds. Florence is astounded, perhaps even more than
on the first day, by this sudden disappearance of the royal
15 family; and the bond of protection that has been improvised
through the force of circumstances between Tuscany and
Sardinia has produced a feeling of distrust and even humili-
ation. Men fear that they will cease to be Tuscan and become
Sardinian; and people who seemed to desire annexation a
20 month ago, out of opposition to the Grand Duke, now appear
anxious to preserve autonomy. M. Boncompagni was saying to
me on this point: 'I have never found my friends so Florentine
as since I have been the King's Commissioner at Florence.'

> Marquis de Ferrières, French ambassador to Tuscany, to
> Count Walewski, 18 May 1859, in D. Beales, *The
> Risorgimento and the Unification of Italy* (London, 1981) p. 166.

(c) *A blueprint for annexation*

If we had proclaimed the annexation of Tuscany to Piedmont
25 three weeks ago, it would perhaps have aroused suspicions in
Europe. But, now that French troops have arrived there with
Prince Napoleon, our annexation will be accepted as a guarantee against possible French ambition in central Italy. At least it
will be thought preferable to republicanism or to being given a
30 ruler from Napoleon's family. Neither in Europe as a whole
nor in Tuscany itself should we encounter any serious obsta-
cles. Most of the local inhabitants will admit that any other
solution is impracticable, and that uncertainty and delay (which

might go on for years) would be dangerous ... I do not mean
35   that you should provoke annexation right away. But you should
arrange with the local authorities to prepare and direct public
opinion toward fusion with us. ... Meanwhile you should
carefully study with the aforesaid authorities what would be
the best method in course of time for testing the national will.
40   Please let me know if and how we can avoid having recourse
to the dangerous expedient of universal suffrage or to the
equally dangerous expedient of an elected assembly. Without
giving you any precise orders, I suggest as one possible idea
that each municipality should individually declare its support
45   for annexation.

> Cavour to Boncompagni, Royal Commissioner in
> Tuscany, 20 May 1859, in D. Mach Smith, *The Making
> of Italy, 1796–1866* (London, 1988) p. 279.

(d) *Alternatives*

28 May Cipriani, who has come from Tuscany, is a partisan for
fusion with Piedmont, but he says that this word 'fusion' has
turned everything in Florence upside down. There is a chaos
of political views. Ridolfi would like a separate ruler chosen
50   from the House of Savoy; Ricasoli wants fusion; Salvagnoli
would prefer Prince Napoleon. There are plenty of partisans
for Tuscan autonomy, and I think that in last analysis this is the
majority view there.

> Massari's diary, in D. Mack Smith, *The Making of Italy,
> 1796–1866* (London, 1988) p. 281.

(e) *French view of events*

The revolution of April 27th had been held within the limits of a
55   certain moderation and I had secured that the provisional government did not declare the Grand Duke deposed or compromise its autonomy. M. Boncompagni had taken the same line;
and the spirit of the people had not developed beyond the habit-
ual calm and mildness of the Tuscans until the arrival of the 5th
60   Corps of the Army of Italy [under Prince Napoleon]. Then followed great pressure from the Piedmontese Government on the
Tuscan Government. The lawyer Salvagnoli entered the Ministry,
and claimed that it was necessary to agitate the country vigorously on behalf of annexation and that this was the Emperor's
65   wish. It was at this date that the revolution really began. ... The
current of the unionist idea dragged the uncertain along with it,
submerged the frightened ... exerting a fascination on people's
minds by its very success. I saw some strange recantations emerge
from informed and important men ... Baron Ricasoli has been
70   the inflexible and unscrupulous agent of this regime of terror,

and there is good reason to be surprised, when one knows the true state of things, that in his last report to M. Boncompagni he should praise the freedom and spontaneity of the municipalities' votes in favour of annexation – since nearly a hundred mayors have been deprived of office and replaced by people of his persuasion, and several municipal councils, including that of Siena … resigned the day after their vote in protest against the violence to which they had been subjected.

> Ferrières to Walewski, 26 July 1859, in D. Beales, *The Risorgimento and the Unification of Italy* (London, 1981) pp. 166–7.

Questions

  a What did Cavour fear in extract (a)?

★ *b* Comment on Boncompagni's change of title, from representative in March to commissioner in May. What had been Piedmont's reaction to the events of 27 April?

★ *c* What was de Ferrières' explanation for the Tuscan desire for autonomy in extract (b)? Explain the last sentence.

★ *d* In extract (c) why did Cavour refer to dangerous expedients (lines 41–42)? What were French troops doing in Tuscany?

  e By late May what were the various alternatives for Tuscany?

★ *f* Identify Baron Ricasoli.

  g To what extent were de Ferrières' accusations of Piedmontese pressure in extract (e) vindicated by extract (c)?

  h Explain de Ferrières' remark in extract (e) that 'it was at this date that the revolution really began.' Is he an objective source?

  i How can these documents be used to support the view that few Tuscans wanted unification in 1859?

---

2 Risings in the Romagna/Legations

(a) *Piedmont's position towards the Legations*

[from a dispatch by Cavour to the Pope, 16 May 1859] Count Cavour while acknowledging the Pope's wishes in terms of high respect, argues that Sardinia, not having troops in the Papal States like France and Austria, is in a different position altogether and cannot bind herself, if certain contingencies arise, to respect the Pope's territory. It may, for

instance, become impossible to allow the Austrians to continue in their present position in the Legations, if they take
advantage of it as a basis of operation against the allied
10   armies. The whole of the country lying between Ancona
and the Po is occupied by them. It is in their power to send
provisions from the Papal States to Lombardy, to impede the
operations about to be undertaken from Tuscany through
Modena, and under such circumstances it might become
15   necessary to drive them out of the Panal States.

        Odo Russell, British representative in Rome, to Earl
        of Malmesbury, Foreign Secretary, 25 May 1859, in
        N. Blakiston (ed.), *The Roman Question* (London, 1961)
        pp. 21–2.

(b) *The Rising*

On the 11th instant the Austrian troops of occupation
received orders from Verona to evacuate the Legations, and
on the 12th they departed without previous notice to the
Papal authorities and proceeded in hurried marches to
20   Ferrara. The immediate result at Bologna and Ravenna was a
rising of the people, the establishment of provisional governments by the municipal authorities and a declaration that the
dictatorship should be offered to King Victor Emmanuel and
an active part taken in the war of independence … Monsieur
25   de Gramont, the French ambassador, condemns and deplores
this popular rising in the Legations in the strongest possible
terms.

        Odo Russell to Earl of Malmesbury, 21 June 1859, in
        N. Blakiston (ed.), *The Roman Question* (London, 1962) pp. 26–7.

(c) *Cavour frustrated*

The whole Romagna cries aloud for the protection and dictatorship of the King, but from Head-quarters I am told –
30   'refuse dictatorship, refuse protection, but accept help for the
war.' This means not to send either d'Azeglio or troops.
What will happen at Bologna when they hear this? Probably
disorder and a violent reaction against the priests …
Gramont and Walewski are complicating matters hopelessly.
35   Gramont … now fulminates against ·the movement at
Bologna and elsewhere. Calls it sacrilege, profanation!
Walewski goes even further, and threatens me with the thun-
ders of heaven!

        Cavour to Prince Napoleon, 21 June 1859, in A. J.
        Whyte, *The Political Life and Letters of Cavour* (Oxford,
        1930) pp. 317–18.

(d) *The French position*

A question which naturally rises into importance at the present
40 moment is, how the Emperor of the French will view the
insurrections which are going on in the Papal States? If he pro-
tects them how can he keep his word to the Pope, and if he
suppresses them by force how can he retain his title as
Liberator of Italy?
45 [Russell's dispatch then includes his memorandum of a
letter, which he was allowed to look at but not copy, from
Napoleon III to Gramont, the French ambassador at Rome,
25 June 1859]. There can exist no contradiction between my
words and my actions. I wish for the independence of Italy,
50 but I must maintain the authority of the Pope in which one
hundred and fifty millions of consciences are interested; and
I am firmly resolved to maintain order in Rome. ... While
on the one hand I refuse to recognise the separation of the
Legations, on the other hand I cannot but appreciate an act
55 which places twenty thousand men at my disposal. But
should the revolution, crossing the Appenines, approach
there where my soldiers are stationed, I could not tolerate if
for one moment.

> Odo Russell to Lord John Russell, 1 July 1859, in
> N. Blakiston (ed.), *The Roman Question* (London,
> 1962) pp. 30–2.

(e) *France reprimands Cavour*

I brought Cavour's attention to the grave and inevitable con-
60 sequences if Piedmont persists in the line of conduct which
she seems to have adopted in Tuscany and the papal
Legations. To this he replied in a way which, as my colleagues at Rome and Florence know well, is as regular with
him as it is *mal à propos*, by assuring me that his policy had
65 been, if not in detail, at least *in general* approved by the
Emperor himself. He added that the Emperor recently con-
gratulated him on the tact and loyalty of Piedmontese policy
in Tuscany. According to Cavour, His Majesty also approved
what had happened in the Legations. The Piedmontese gov-
70 ernment therefore cannot understand how our ambassador at
Rome, who must know the Emperor's mind, should be so
surprised. ... If Cavour has shown little inclination to help us
in Tuscany, he is even less trustworthy in the Legations. This
area has long been coveted by Piedmont and is now the main
75 preoccupation of her statesmen. England, for obvious
reasons, does not discourage this. It cost Cavour a great deal
to have to renounce the policy of annexation and dictatorship by Piedmont which he had stated and promised in

advance. But in the last resort he is sure that the Emperor
80 will give him these provinces when the time comes for a
final settlement; and meanwhile he continues to keep up the
expectations of the local population.

> La Tour d'Auvergne, French ambassador in Turin, to
> Walewski, 3 July 1859, in D. Mack Smith, *The Making
> of Italy, 1796–1866* (London, 1988) pp. 284–5.

Questions

a Why was the geographical position of the Legations
important?

b What reasons did Cavour give for possible intervention?

★ c What battle caused the Austrian troops to evacuate the
Legations in mid-June? Why should the French
ambassador have condemned the rising?

d In extract (c) explain 'Head-quarters'.

e What did Cavour fear if the Legations were not brought
under Piedmont's authority? How reliable are his
assertions in extract (c)?

f In extract (d) how did Napoleon attempt to resolve the
French dilemma concerning the risings in the Legations?

g In what way did Cavour counter French accusations of
his conduct in the Legations?

h Is there a hint of differing opinions between Napoleon III
and his representatives in Italy?

3   French withdrawal: Villafranca

(a) *An opinion of French assistance,* Punch, *11 June 1859*

THE GIANT AND THE DWARF.

"BRAVO, MY LITTLE FELLOW! YOU SHALL DO ALL THE FIGHTING, AND WE'LL DIVIDE THE GLORY!"

Questions

a Identify the two men.
b Do the events of this month of June 1859 tend to
   confirm or deny the cartoonist's opinion of the giant's
   view?
c What does this cartoon tell you about the attitude of the
   British public to this episode of the *Risorgimento*?

(b) The terms of Villafranca

1. The Emperors of Austria and France will favour the creation of an Italian Confederation under the honorary Presidency of the Holy Father.
2. The Emperor of Austria cedes to the Emperor of France all his rights upon Lombardy, except the fortresses of Mantua and Peschiera. The Emperor of France will hand over this territory to the King of Sardinia. Venice will form part of the Confederation remaining in the possession of Austria.
3. The Grand Duke of Tuscany and the Duke of Modena will return to their States proclaiming a general amnesty.
4. The two Emperors will ask the Holy Father to introduce into his States indispensable reforms.

> Peace of Villafranca, 11 July 1859, in A. J. Whyte, *The Political Life and Letters of Cavour* (Oxford, 1930) p. 325.

(c) Cavour obdurate

Just as Cavour was declaiming against the King and everyone else, the door opened and Prince Jerome Napoleon entered. He took part in the discussion which was embittered by his abrupt rudeness. Cavour declined to entertain the idea of a prolonged armistice, or of treating for peace, save under the condition of the liberating of northern Italy – from the Alps to the Adriatic – as announced by Napoleon III. The Prince replied that we ought to be only too pleased to get Lombardy and the Duchies. I remember he wound up by exclaiming, 'Do you expect us to sacrifice France and our dynasty for you?' Cavour doggedly replied that promises were promises, and ought to be kept. He threatened to promote and head a revolution rather than leave the work half done, and complained bitterly of the Emperor, of the King, of La Marmora, of me ... Cavour, as a last resource, wished to carry on the war alone; but 1848 was too fresh in our memories, and, as military men, we declined the responsibility. ... But Cavour would not listen to argument, and finding the King, the Emperor, and Prince Jerome Napoleon inexorable, resigned and left for Turin.

> Report by Piedmontese Chief of Staff, in R. L. H. Lloyd, *Cavour and Italian Unification, 1854–80* (London, 1975) pp. 43–4.

(d) Cavour intemperate

The terms of this peace shall never be carried out! This treaty shall never be executed! I will take Solaro della Margherita by one hand and Mazzini by the other, if need be. I will turn conspirator. I will become a revolutionary.

> Cavour at his meeting with Kossuth, 14 July 1859, in A. J. Whyte, *The Political Life and Letters of Cavour* (Oxford, 1930) p. 327.

Questions

a   In extract (b) who was the 'Holy Father' (line 3)?

★ b   Why was Parma ignored in the treaty; what was to be its fate?

c   Which of the terms confirmed Plombières, and which differed?

★ d   What were the nature of the reforms which the powers hoped to see introduced in the Papal States?

e   Which of the terms were most unlikely to be implemented?

f   In extract (c) identify 'Duchies' (line 22).

g   Why was Prince Napoleon so aggrieved?

h   What did Cavour mean by threatening to head a revolution in extracts (c) and (d)? Explain the mention of Mazzini.

i   Why did Cavour feel it necessary to resign?

(e) *The Peace explained to the French army*

Soldiers – the bases of a peace have been agreed on with the Emperor of Austria; the principal object of the war is attained; Italy will for the first time become a nation. A Confederation of all the States of Italy under the honorary Presidency of the
5   Pope will reunite in one group the members of the same family. Venice, it is true, will remain under the sceptre of Austria, but it will be, nevertheless, an Italian province forming part of the Confederation.

The union of Lombardy to Piedmont creates for us on this
10   side of the Alps a powerful ally, who will owe to us his independence ... [French troops have been uniformly successful] and have only stopped because the conflict was assuming a magnitude no longer in proportion to the interests that France had in this formidable war.

> From the *Moniteur*, 12 July 1859, in R. L. H. Lloyd, *Cavour and Italian Unification, 1854–60* (London, 1975), pp. 45–6.

(f) *Unofficial French reasons*

15   If annexation crossed the Appenines, unity would be made, and I do not wish to see unity. I want only independence. Unity would bring danger to me in France itself, because of

the Roman question, and France would not see with pleasure a
great nation armed on her flank which might diminish her
20   preponderance.

> Napoleon III to Marquis Pepoli, 15 July 1859, in
> A. J. Whyte, *The Political Life and Letters of Cavour*
> (Oxford, 1980) p. 332.

(g) *The British view*

I infer that what put the finishing stroke to the war was
Massimo d'Azgelio's mission to Bologna. As soon as the
Emperor saw, or fancied he saw, that he was being made a tool
for Sardinian projects, he determined to cut short these
25   intrigues by making peace.

> Lord Cowley to Lord John Russell, 28 July 1859, in
> R. L. H. Lloyd, *Cavour and Italian Unification, 1854–60*
> (London, 1975) p. 46.

(h) *The Church's response*

As to the Italian Confederation, it is a beautiful idea … but the
obstacle to a Confederation must be sought in the impossibility to
establish a sincere union between the people and their governments, and how can Naples, Tuscany and Austria live on terms of
30   friendship with Piedmont, who is ever at work to set the People
against their Rulers? And again, how is Austria to behave as a
member of both the Italian and Germanic Confederations, should
the two powers ever go to war with each other? … In short the
difficulties appear almost insurmountable but His Holiness is ready
35   to accept the Protectorate if the Confederation can be organised.

> Cardinal Antonelli, Papal Secretary of State, as reported
> by Odo Russell to Lord John Russell, 23 November
> 1859, in N. Blakiston (ed.), *The Roman Question*
> (London, 1962) pp. 63–4.

Questions

a   Identify and account for any differences between extracts
   (e) and (f).
b   Explain Napoleon's distinction between unity and
   independence.
★ c   Define the Roman Question.
d   How accurate is extract (g) in the light of extract (f)?
e   Summarise the reasons which led Napoleon III to
   negotiate the peace at Villafranca.
f   How valid were Antonelli's points concerning the
   proposed Confederation? What was the 'Germanic
   Confederation'?

4 Central Italy goes it alone

(a) *Farini continues the pressure*

The Preliminaries of Villafranca left Modena once again to create
her own government. I agreed to become Dictator as I was
unable to refuse the pressing invitation made to me by the various
town councils. But I promised to convoke a National Assembly
5   to set up a legitimate authority and give voice to the political
wishes of the people. Speedily putting this into practice, I published an edict giving the vote to all literate citizens, for this
would show a genuine popular will while at the same time paying
regard to the political and social condition of the country ...
10 By now you will have heard of the unanimous decisions of
the National Assembly of the Modenese Provinces ... [which]
proclaimed annexation of the Modenese Provinces to the
Kingdom of Piedmont–Sardinia under the constitutional
sceptre of our valiant and loyal King Victor Emmanual. ...
15 A defensive alliance has now been signed between Modena
and Tuscany. The government of the Romagna has asked to
join it, and this has been agreed. The alliance will be completed by the accession of the Duchy of Parma and Piacenza.
This League has, as its first aim, to unite Tuscany, the
20 Modenese Provinces, Parma and Piacenza in resisting the
restoration of their deposed dynasties, and to defend the papal
Legations against any attack by the mercenaries of the
pontifical government.

> Diplomatic circular by L. Farini, 25 August 1859, in
> D. Mack Smith, *The Making of Italy, 1796–1866*
> (London, 1988) pp. 292–4.

(b) *French condemnation*

Piedmont is setting herself up as the representative and protec-
25 tor of the Assemblies which now exist in central Italy, but she
cannot conceal that these Assemblies have been elected and
summoned in exceptional circumstances which hardly guarantee a free and reliable vote. ...
The French government sets a high value on the expression
30 of popular will, for it bases its own strength on this very thing,
but equally one must take other facts into account, for instance
questions of expediency, promises made, or rights previously
acquired. The treaty of Villafranca, by giving Lombardy to
Piedmont, opened in fact what was a new era for Italy. ... But
35 it will endanger the other results of that settlement if Piedmont
tries to precipitate events and extends its terms unduly.
Every contract, by its very nature as a contract, implies give
as well as take, and it is wrong to repudiate contractual obliga-

tions once you have gained from them. The preliminaries
40   agreed at Villafranca, and the treaty negotiations at Zurich, at
the same time as they gave Lombardy to Piedmont, allow the
sovereigns of the central Italian states to return to their thrones
with their old rights intact. The two things are connected. If
Piedmont opposes the return of these sovereigns (or if she so
45   much as countenances the possibility of annexing central Italy),
that would nullify the cession of Lombardy.

> Walewski to French ambassador in Piedmont,
> 12 October 1859, in R. L. H. Lloyd, *Cavour and Italian
> Unification, 1854–60* (London, 1975) pp. 48–9.

Questions

★   *a*   Identify Farini.
   b   Was his first sentence accurate? How did it differ from
        the interpretation of Villafranca in extract (b)?
★   *c*   Why did Farini insist on voting restrictions in Modena?
   d   Why was Venetia not included in this new central Italian
        group?
   e   In extract (b) explain Walewski's comment 'for it bases its
        own strength on this very thing' (line 30).
   f   What was the nature of Walewski's threat to Piedmont?

---

5   French acquiescence: the bargain struck

(a)   *The Papacy reviews Napoleon's volte-face*

I called yesterday on the Cardinal Secretary of State in order to
learn the opinion of the Papal Government on the pamphlet
lately published, *Le Pape et le Congrès*.

   'We know not,' Cardinal Antonelli said, 'and care not who is
5   the author of that pamphlet, but since the government of the
Emperor saw fit to take measures against the circulation of the
charges of the French Bishops to the clergy of their dioceses and
against the Catholic newspapers who were writing in favour of
the Pope, I have deemed it my duty to demand of the French
10   Ambassador here, since Count Walewski was unable to give satis-
factory explanation to our Nuncio at Paris, how the publication
of a pamphlet directed against the Pope and the Holy See could
have been permitted by the French Government. As to the principles contained in that pamphlet, they are revolutionary and
15   dangerous to the peace of Europe, for where, I ask, is a system to
end, which advocates taking the lawful property of one person to
give it to another and which totally ignores the principles of

equity and of international law. ... If the Pope himself were to
say to me: prepare the cession of the Romagna, I should resign
20   my charge into his hands and say: Holy Father! Neither you nor
I, nor anyone else has a right to do it. ... The Church can never
cede any portion of her states.

> Odo Russell to Lord John Russell, 4 January 1859, in
> N. Blakiston (ed.), *The Roman Question* (London, 1962)
> pp. 74–6.

(b) *Cavour resurgent*

The prorogation of the Congress, the publication of the
brochure, the Emperor's letter to the Pope, and his *rapproche-*
25   *ment* with England, these four facts, of which the least important would have been sufficient to precipitate the solution of
pending questions, have rendered any longer delay impossible.
Fully commented on by the European Press, they have convinced all serious minds that (i) all idea of the restoration of the
30   dispossessed rulers must be given up: it is as impossible now at
Bologna and Parma as at Florence and Modena. (ii) The only
possible solution lies in the legal admission of annexation,
already established in fact both in Emilia and Tuscany. (iii) The
Italian populations, having waited in vain for Europe to settle
35   their affairs upon the basis of non-intervention and respect for
popular opinion, have now the duty of going forward and pro-
viding for their own government.

> Circular by Cavour to his diplomatic agents, 27 January
> 1860, in A. J. Whyte, *The Political Life and Letters of
> Cavour* (Oxford, 1930) pp. 347–8.

Questions

★ *a* Who was supposed to have instigated this pamphlet?
From extract (a) what can be deduced about its import?

★ *b* Explain the reasons for the French change of attitude.
What was the fate of Walewski?

    c Florence and Bologna were the capitals of which regions?

    d In extract (b) what was 'the brochure' (lines 23–24)?

★ *e* What was Emilia? How had it been formed? Why was
there no effective resistance from the Papal government?

(c) *The price*

As to the Emperor of France, after his famous pamphlet he has
shut himself in an impenetrable silence, and has made it plain
that he does not want any more deputations from Central Italy.
I do not expect that he will be in favour of annexation. On the

5   contrary, I believe that he would wish us not to do it, and truly
      the pledges given at Villafranca make it impossible for him to
      sanction it. I must assure myself that he will not oppose us too
      resolutely. It is necessary to study him, to probe his mind, and
      observe his attitude to us. What I am resolved to do, whatever
10   happens, is to admit the deputies of Central Italy to Parliament.
      ... The knot of the question appears to be neither the
      Romagna nor Tuscany, but Savoy. ... Though I have received
      no communication of any kind on this subject, either from
      Paris or Turin, though Talleyrand has assured me that he had
15   instructions not to speak of Savoy and Nice, I have understood
      that we have been on the wrong road and I am trying to give
      our policy a different direction.

> Cavour to Giorgini in late January, in A. J. Whyte, *The
> Political Life and Letters of Cavour* (Oxford, 1930)
> pp. 345–6.

(d) *The cession of Savoy and Nice to France*

      The Sardinian Government has consented to the demand of
      France to effect the cession of Savoy and Nice by a special
20   treaty to be concluded between France and Piedmont. The
      treaty will be followed by a vote of the municipalities con-
      cerned, and the two Contracting Parties will afterwards com-
      municate to the European Powers the nature of, and motives
      for, the territorial arrangements between them.

> From *The Times*, 16 March 1860, in R. L. H. Lloyd,
> *Cavour and Italian Unification, 1854–60* (London, 1975)
> p. 49.

(e) *Motives*

25   *24 March* The cession of Savoy and Nice appears to be an
      inescapable necessity if we are to remain allied to Napoleon;
      the French are here acting with a military ruthlessness that
      Piedmont finds offensive. But Cavour, by giving Napoleon this
      bone to gnaw, against the wish of Europe, hopes to bind him
30   indissolubly to the cause of Italy. We shall see who wins in this
      war of wits.

> Diary of M. Tabarrini, in D. Mack Smith, *The Making of
> Italy, 1796–1856* (London, 1988) p. 303.

(f) *British chagrin*

      Cavour not only concealed the undertaking he had made over
      Savoy before the war of 1859, but he recently told us once
      again that he had not the slightest intention of ceding,
35   exchanging or selling Savoy. All his talk of plebiscites, votes

and parliamentary decisions is a farce. Cavour's surrender of these provinces is iniquitous, especially as it was unnecessary. The Emperor would never have dared face the condemnation of Europe; or, if he had, Count Cavour would have been
40   acclaimed for honesty as much as for his courage and skill.

From a conversation of Palmerston to Panizzi, in E. d'Azeglio to Cavour, 14 April 1860, in R. L. H. Lloyd, *Cavour and Italian Unification, 1854–60* (London, 1975) p. 50.

Questions

a To what parliament was Cavour referring in extract (c)?
b Explain the last sentence of extract (c).
c Were Savoy and Nice largely French or Italian speaking respectively?
d Explain 'a vote of the municipalities concerned' in extract (d).
★ e Why should Europe have opposed the cession of Savoy and Nice?
★ f Why did Palmerston think Cavour's talk of plebiscites, votes and parliamentary decisions a farce? How would Cavour have responded to the general British accusations in extract (f)?

VII   Southern Unification

Introduction

In April 1860 a revolt took place in Sicily against the Bourbon rulers of the island. It seemed to have been put down when Garibaldi sailed from Genoa to Marsala in western Sicily with barely one thousand irregulars. He proceeded to defeat the greatly superior Neapolitan forces in an engagement in May, occupy Palermo, and drive the Bourbons out of Sicily. In August he crossed over to Calabria and advanced up the toe of Italy until he entered Naples on 7 September, King Francis II having hastily removed himself the day before.

In Piedmont, meanwhile, there was not unqualified pleasure at this sequence of events. At the outset Garibaldi's aims were unclear. It was not until the expedition to Sicily was under way that he announced his forces would be acting on behalf of Victor Emmanuel and 'Italy'. Although this removed the threat of a republic (and Garibaldi had started his career as a Mazzinian), it suggested that not only would Garibaldi strive to topple the Bourbons in the Kingdom of the Two Sicilies, but also he would go on to attack the Papal States, then protected by French troops, and even Venetia, still an Austrian province. In addition there was the danger of independent conduct, with Garibaldi encouraging reforms, such as the abolition of feudalism in Sicily, which nervous conservative factions in the north might read as social revolution.

Historians have disagreed about Cavour's policy during these months from April to September. The traditional view is that secretly he supported Garibaldi's venture, but was unable to do so openly, nor offer any substantial aid, for fear of alienating France and risking war with Austria. More recently, it has been asserted that Cavour genuinely wanted to stop Garibaldi's expedition; tried to prevent him from crossing the straits to the Neapolitan mainland; and planned a contained revolution in Naples which would pre-empt Garibaldi's more extreme movement. If these were his intensions they certainly failed, and Cavour was forced to compromise and adapt his policies in line with rapidly developing events. Each month seemed to bring a subtle change in direction; one reason alone why the precise dating of these documents is vital.

Finally there was the position of Victor Emmanuel. The King got on far better with Garibaldi than with his chief minister and there is evidence that he pursued an individual policy from that of Cavour. The exact nature of this attitude is obscure, however, and the surviving documents sometimes contradictory.

1   Reactions to the Sicilian Rising

(a) *Mazzini encourages his supporters in Sicily*

Brothers! ... I confess I no longer recognise in the Sicilians of today the men who flung down the challenge in 48.... First of all I repeat to you our declaration of two years ago. It is no longer a question of Republic or Monarchy; it is ques-
5 tion of National Unity, of existence or non-existence.... If Italy wishes to be a monarchy under the House of Savoy, let it be so. If, at the end, they choose to hail the King and Cavour as liberators or what not, let it be so. What we all will is that Italy shall be made; and if she is to be made, she
10 must be made by her own inspiration and conscience, and not by giving a free hand, as to methods, to Cavour and the King, while we remain inert and wait. Wait for what? In good faith, can you believe that Cavour, the King and L. Napoleon will come to give you liberty? ... Cavour has
15 only a single aim – to add Venetia to the Monarchy, as was agreed at Plombières. L. Napoleon has only a single aim: to secure Savoy and maintain French supremacy in Italy... . Fixed in his single purpose, Cavour does not desire new complications. L. Napoleon fears them. Neither from one
20 nor the other, therefore, can you expect salvation ... Garibaldi is bound to aid... . For heaven's sake, dare! You will be followed. But dare in the name of National Unity; it is the condition *sine qua non*. Dare: summon to power a little nucleus of energetic men; let their first acts speak of Italy, of
25 the Nation; let them call on the Italians of the Centre and of the North. You will have them.

> Guiseppe Mazzini, 2 March 1860, quoted in G. M. Trevelyan, *Garibaldi and the Thousand* (London, 1909) pp. 145–6.

(b) *Cavour comments on the proposed expedition*

I have reason to believe that H. M., who has a weakness for
Garibaldi and Rattazzi, is secretly looking to remove me
from the direction of affairs.... In [Genoa] the Mazzinian
30 agitation is regaining strength and is rallying around
Garibaldi. There is a desire to force the Government to
come to the aid of Sicily, and expeditions of arms and muni-
tions are being prepared. I suspect the King of imprudently
favouring these projects. I have given orders for a close
35 watch to be kept and to stop – if that is possible – these des-
perate endeavours.

> Cavour to Nigra, 24 April 1860, in A. J. Whyte, *The
> Political Life and Letters of Cavour* (Oxford, 1930) p. 391.

(c) *Garibaldi explains his actions before sailing*

Tell His Majesty not to be angry with me for I am truly his
friend for life. If I had told him my plans he would have put
a stop to them; and hence, regretfully, I preferred to keep
40 silent. I opposed this rising in Sicily; but when those fine
Italians took action on their own I had to help them. Assure
His Majesty that, whatever happens, the honour of Italy will
not suffer.

> Garibaldi to Marquis Trecchi, an aide to the King,
> 4 May 1860, in D. Mack Smith, *The Making of Italy,
> 1796–1866* (London, 1988) p. 308.

(d) *The Press on Garibaldi's motives*

Garibaldi, in his private letters, expresses real regret that he
45 was obliged to leave without paying his respects to the King.
It would have been impossible to conceal his design from the
King, and he did not wish to put his resolution to the test of
the winning manners of that Victor Emmanuel whose
earnest entreaty had already the power to dissuade him from
50 another of his bold schemes – the invasion of the Marches a
few months ago. His profession of devotion and attachment
to the King are both warm and cordial, and he inveighs
against his pusillanimous Ministers in no measured terms.
There are men about me who think all his indignation is put
55 on, and that there is a collusion between the projector of the
expedition, and those who affect to condemn and take
apparent measures to thwart it; but such people, I believe,
only betray their ignorance of Garibaldi's character, [and]
were not probably present at the sitting in the Chamber at
60 the time of the famous Garibaldi *interpellation* on the subject
of Nice. Cavour wounded the brave Nizzard there.

From *The Times*, 14 May 1860, in R. L. Lloyd, *Cavour and Italian Unification, 1854–60* (London, 1975) p. 51.

(e) *Three different memories of Cavour's attitude to the expedition*

(i) Next I ask the hon. General Sirtori to tell the Chamber what answer he got from Count Cavour when he went to see him two evenings before [23 April] on his return from the festivities in Tuscany ... [Cavour] said, 'I don't know what to say or what to do,' and, in the sly way he had, ended, rubbing his hands, 'I think they will be taken.'

> Dr Bertani, in Italian Parliament, 19 June 1863, from G. M. Trevelyan, *Garibaldi and the Thousand* (London, 1909) p. 301.

(ii) As to the expedition to the Marches, [Cavour] said absolutely: 'No: the government will oppose it by every means in its power.' As to the expedition to Sicily, Cavour said exactly these words: 'Well and good. Begin at the south, to come up again by the north. When it is a question of undertakings of that kind, however bold they may be, Count Cavour will be second to none.' These were his precise words. He said this naturally referring to all those means by which the government without compromising itself could help the expedition. He promised to help it, provided the responsibility of the government was completely concealed.

> Guiseppe Sirtori, in Italian Parliament, 19 June 1863, from G. M. Trevelyan, *Garibaldi and the Thousand* (London, 1909) p. 174.

(iii) ... at the outset nobody believed in the possibility of Garibaldi's success, and Cavour, and *tutti quanti*, thought the country well rid of him and of the unquiet spirits who went with him. The argument was, if he fails we are rid of a troublesome fellow, and if he succeeds Italy will derive some profit from this success.

> Sir James Hudson to Lord John Russell, 28 June 1860, quoted in D. Mack Smith, *Victor Emmanuel, Cavour and the Risorgimento* (Oxford, 1971) pp. 181–2.

   a Explain references in extract (a) to the 'challenge in 48' (line 2) and 'as was agreed at Plombières' (lines 15–16).

   b Why should Mazzini have referred to L. Napoleon and not Napoleon III or the Emperor?

   c Can extract (a) be used to support the view that Mazzini was prepared to abandon republicanism for the sake of unity?

★ *d* Was Mazzini right in his predictions of (i) Cavour, (ii) Napoleon, (iii) Garibaldi?

★ *e* Why should the king have been wanting to get rid of Cavour?

   f Explain the last sentence of extract (d).

   g To what extent does extract (c) confirm extract (d)?

   h In extract (e) what did Bertani imply in his recollection (part i)?

   i In extract (e) what does 'begin at the south … north' mean (part ii, lines 67–8)?

★ *j* In extract (e) why should Cavour have supported the Sicilian expedition but not one to the Marches (part ii)?

   k In the light of all these extracts, which version of Cavour's attitude to Garibaldi's expedition given in extract (e) (parts i and ii) is more convincing? Account for the difference.

2   The expedition sails

(a) *Garibaldi defines his objective en route to Sicily*

The mission of this corps will depend, as it did before, on the most complete self-sacrifice, for the regeneration of our fatherland … now that the hour of strife has come again, once more Italy sees them in the foremost rank, joyful, willing, and ready
5 to shed their blood for her. The present war cry … shall be the same as that which rang out along the banks of the Ticino, twelve months ago, – ITALY AND VICTOR EMMANUEL. And wherever we shall utter this war-cry it will strike terror to the hearts of all enemies of Italy.

> Garibaldi's proclamation, 7 May 1860, in T. Palamenghi-Crispi (ed.), *The Memoirs of Francesco Crispi* (London, 1912) p. 169.

(b) *Cavour sends orders concerning the expedition*

10 Garibaldi has embarked with 400 volunteers on two Rubattino
steamers for Sicily. If he enters a port of Sardinia arrest the
expedition. I authorize you to employ, if required, the
squadron commanded by Count Persano.

[Next day he sent a further explanatory telegram]:

15 Do not arrest the expedition out at sea. Only if it enters a
port.

> Cavour's telegram to Governor of Cagliari in Sardinia,
> 7 and 8 May 1860, quoted in G. M. Trevelyan, *Garibaldi
> and the Thousand* (London, 1909) p. 206.

(c) *Persano interprets these orders*

9 May: I must arrest the volunteers departed from Genoa for
Sicily on two packet steamers of the Rubbatino Company
under the command of General Garibaldi wherever they put
into in Sardinia. BUT I MUST LET THEM PROCEED ON
20 THEIR WAY IF I MEET THEM AT SEA. I asked to be
telegraphed 'CAGLIARI' if they really wanted me to stop it,
and 'MALTA' in the opposite case, leaving to Cavour the
opportunity of giving me total responsibility.

11 May: Count Cavour telegraphs me. The MINISTRY has
25 decided for CAGLIARI – This indicated to me that the decision has been taken by the Ministry, giving me to understand
that he, Cavour, thought differently; and so, to put him at his
ease, I hasten to reply – 'I have understood' – and resolve to let
the daring soldier of fortune proceed to his destiny.

> Admiral Persano's diary for 1860–1, published in 1869,
> in *Navale, 1860–61* (Florence, 1869) 1, pp. 14–15.

(d) *Cavour defends himself*

30 I regret Garibaldi's expedition as much as does Monsieur
Thouvenel [the French Foreign Minister], and I am doing,
and will go on doing, everything possible to prevent it
causing new complications. I did not prevent Garibaldi
carrying out his project, because that would have needed
35 force. Moreover the government is in no state to face up to
the enormous unpopularity which we would have incurred
by arresting Garibaldi. Another consideration was that elec-
tions were imminent, and I need the support of all shades of
the moderate liberal party if we are to foil the intrigues of
40 the opposition and get the French treaty passed. Therefore I
could not take vigorous action to prevent help being sent to
Sicily. But I did everything in my power to persuade
Garibaldi not to go on his mad escapade. I sent La Farina to

talk to him, who came back with an assurance that the
45 whole idea was off.

As we had news from Palermo that the Bourbons had
lifted martial law and that the insurrection there had almost
died out, I thought Garibaldi would be obliged to stay put
whether he liked it or not. I could never have dreamt that he
50 was mad enough to land in Umbria where Generals
Lamoricière and Goyon had forces far superior to his own.
This is surely convincing proof that we are not conniving
with Garibaldi; for no one will think me so mad as to want a
revolution in Umbria at the present moment. As I commu-
55 nicated to you by telegraph, I had already given orders to
Rear-Admiral Persano to arrest Garibaldi in Sardinian
waters. And yesterday, as soon as I heard that some of his followers had landed at Talamone [in Tuscany], I gave orders
for his ships to be stopped wherever they were, except in the
60 waters of the Kingdom of the Two Sicilies (the King of
Naples has no need for our help for his own policing). Please
explain all this to M. Thouvenel.

> Cavour to Nigra, 12 May 1860, in D. Mack Smith, *The
> Making of Italy, 1796–1866* (London, 1938) pp. 308–9.

(e) *Arming the expedition*

It was unanimously decided to refuse Garibaldi the guns he
requires for the Sicilian insurrection, lest the European capitals
65 should thereby be alarmed, in view of the imprudent publicity
given by him as his friends in Genoa to the preparations he has
in hand in Sicily. It was also resolved that any meeting of the
émigrés in Genoa should be forbidden.

> Piedmontese cabinet minute, 24 April 1860, quoted in
> D. Mack Smith, *Victor Emmanuel, Cavour and the
> Risorgimento* (Oxford, 1971) p. 184.

(f) *Garibaldi looks back at the events of April–May 1860*

Every possible obstacle was raised in our path [by Cavour and
70 the Piedmontese government] … Some people try to argue
that the government could have stopped us and yet let us go,
but I deny that they could have stopped us. Public opinion was
irresistibly on our side from the first moment that news spread
of the Sicilian rising in April 1860. It is true that the govern-
75 ment put no absolute veto in our way [Garibaldi here wrote,
and then crossed out, 'hoping to be rid forever of a lot of trou-
blemakers like us']; nevertheless they raised every kind of
obstacle. I was not allowed to take any of the 15,000 muskets
which belonged to our Million Rifle Fund and were kept by
80 us in storage at Milan. This one fact delayed by several days the

sailing of our expedition. La Farina then gave us just 1,000 bad firearms and 8,000 lire.

> Garibaldi's memoirs, published in 1908, from D. Mack Smith (ed.), *Garibaldi: A Portrait in Documents* (Florence, 1982) pp. 30–1.

Questions

a What is the significance of no numeral after the King's name in Garibaldi's proclamation? Explain 'Ticino, twelve months ago'.

★ b Why did this proclamation dismay a number of Garibaldi's men; and what did they do?

c In what way is Persano's impression of Cavour's thinking contradicted by the other documents? Account for the differences.

★ d What were Cavour's confessed reasons for not stopping the expedition? In extract (d) explain the French treaty (line 40).

★ e Who were the Generals mentioned in extract (d)? What respective troops did they command?

f Why is extract (e) of particular reliability for historians? Do extracts (d) and (f) essentially agree on events?

g To what extent did Cavour's trust of Nigra, and the latter's posting during these years, make this letter at once more *and* less reliable?

h How could these documents be used to prove (i) that Cavour helped the expedition, (ii) that Cavour hindered the expedition?

---

3 Success in Sicily: difficulties for Cavour

(a) *A Sicilian aristocrat (apolitical but with faint liberal sympathies) considers the alternatives shortly before Garibaldi's arrival*

And as he exchanged gossip with the impeccable chamberlain he was asking himself what was destined to succeed this monarchy [of Naples] which bore the marks of death upon its face. The Piedmontese, the so-called *Galantuomo* who was
5 getting himself so talked of from that little out-of-the-way capital of his? Wouldn't things be just the same? Just Torinese instead of Neapolitan dialect; that's all.

He had reached for the book. He signed: Fabrizio Corbera, Prince of Salina.

10   Or maybe the Republic of Don Peppino Mazzini? 'No thanks I'd just be plain Signor Corbera.' ... This being the case then, what should he do? Just cling to the status quo and avoid leaps in the dark? Then he would have to put up with more rattle of firing squads like that which had resounded a short
15   time before through a squalid square in Palermo; and what use were they, anyway? 'One never achieves anything by going bang! bang! Does one Bendico [the Prince's dog]?'

'Ding! Ding! Ding!' rang the bell for dinner. Bendico rushed ahead with mouth watering in anticipation. 'Just like a
20   Piedmontese!' thought Salina as he moved back up the steps.

[Later the Prince reads about Garibaldi's landing]

'On the 11th May an act of flagrant piracy culminated in the landing of armed men at Marsala. The latest reports that the band numbers about eight hundred, and is commanded by
25   Garibaldi. When these brigands set foot on land they were very careful to avoid any encounter with the royal troops, and moved off, as far as can be ascertained, in the direction of Castelvetrano, threatening peaceful citizens and spreading rapine and devastation, etc., etc ... '
30   The name of Garibaldi disturbed him a little. That adventurer all hair and beard was a pure Mazzinian. He had caused a lot of trouble already. 'But if that *Galantuomo* King of his has let him come down here it means they're sure of him. They'll curb him!'

From the novel by G. Tomasi di Lampedusa, *The Leopard* (London, 1988 edn) pp. 32–3, 53–4.

(b) *One of Garibaldi's expeditionary force describes the battle of Calatafimi*

16 May, above Calatafimi ... We got to our feet, closed up and
35   rushed like a flash down to the plain below. There we came under a perfect hail of bullets, while from the smoke-wreathed mountain two guns began a furious cannonade against us.

The plain was quickly crossed and the first enemy line was broken, but when we came to the slopes of the opposite hill it
40   was not pleasant to look upwards. I saw Garibaldi on foot with his sheathed sword over his right shoulder, walking slowly forward, keeping the whole action in view. Our men were falling all around him and it seemed that those who wore the red shirt were the most numerous victims ... I begun to fear that the
45   General thought it impossible that we could win this fight, and that he was therefore seeking death on the battlefield ...

The first, second, and third terraces up the hillside were attacked at the point of the bayonet and passed, but it was terrible to see the dead and wounded. Little by little, as they
50   yielded ground, the royalist battalions retreated higher up ...

we could hear ... thousands of voices like waves of an angry sea, shouting from time to time, 'Long live the King!'

> G. C. Abba, *The Diary of One of Garibaldi's Thousand* (London, 1962) pp. 30, 35–7.

(c) Garibaldi introduces social reform

[As well as measures dealing with land distribution and popular education] Garibaldi, in virtue of the powers conferred on
55 him, and acting on the principle that a free people should change any of its customs which derive from a previous era of slavery, decrees:

> Article 1 No one shall any longer address other people as 'Your Excellency.'
60 Article 2 The *baciamano* [by which a serf would kiss the hand of his landlord] is henceforth illegal.
> Signed, G. Garibaldi and F. Crispi

> > Decree of the Dictator of Sicily, 13 June 1860, in D. Mack Smith (ed.), *Garibaldi* (Florence, 1982) p. 30.

(d) Garibaldi insufficiently radical for some

22 May, still at Parco [A young friar explains to one of the thousand why he could not join the insurgents]
65 'I should have come, if I were only sure that you were on some great mission, but I have spoken with many of your comrades and the only thing they could say to me was that you wish to unite Italy.'

'Certainly we do, to make one great people.'
70 'You mean, one territory; as far as the people are concerned, one or many, they are bound to suffer and they go on suffering and I have not heard that you want to make them happy.'

'Of course! The people will have liberty and education –'

'Is that all?' broke in the friar. 'Liberty is not bread, nor is
75 education. Perhaps these things suffice for you Piedmontese but not for us here.'

'Well. What do you want then?'

'War! We want war, not war against the Bourbons only, but against all oppressors, great and small, who are not only to be
80 found at curt but in every city, in every hamlet.'

> G. C. Abba, *The Diary of One of Garibaldi's Thousand* (London, 1962) p. 54.

(e) Crispi anatomises his fellow Sicilians

There are none here who are truly Unionists from principle, save your friend and the handful of young men who follow me. The country in general is indifferent; the people hate the Bourbons because they were tortured by them, but they take no thought of how best to get rid of them, or of what form of government is to take their place. Among the men of 1848, through whom the country was lost at that time, there is not one who is really in favour of national union. They pretend to wish to see Sicily united to the other Italian provinces that have been emancipated, but in their hearts they are casting about for an excuse to change sides, and demand a prince for Palermo. The marvelous achievements of Garibaldi's expedition, and my rapid organisation of the country, forced this party to remain silent. But now La Farina has sown discord throughout this unhappy land … by launching the filthy and cowardly accusation of republicanism against us.

F. Crispi to C. Correnti, 5 July 1860, in T. Palamanghi-Crispi (ed.), *The Memoirs of Francesco Crispi* (London, 1912) p. 304.

(f) *Cavour fears Garibaldi's intentions*

Garibaldi has become intoxicated by success and by the praise showered on him from all over Europe. He is planning the wildest, not to say absurdest, schemes. As he remains devoted to King Victor Emmanuel, he will not help Mazzini or republicanism. But he feels it his vocation to liberate all Italy, stage by stage, before turning her over to the King. He is thus putting off the day when Sicily will demand annexation to Piedmont, for he wants to keep the dictatorial powers which will enable him to raise an army to conquer first Naples, then Rome, and in the end Venice. Some people even maintain that in private conversation he does not conceal his intention of taking Nice back from France! But I find that too hard to believe.

The government here has no influence on him. On the contrary he mistrusts everybody whom he imagines to be in touch with us. La Farina has been treated in a disgraceful way, first isolated, then expelled from Sicily without the slightest reason, and everyone has been dismissed who tried to interfere …

The King still retains some influence over him, but if he tried using it on this occasion he would lose it to no purpose. That would be a grave misfortune, as circumstances could arise in which the King's influence would be our only hope… . We must therefore prevent Garibaldi from conquering Naples, and we must try and annex Sicily as soon as possible.

Were Garibaldi to become master of all the Neapolitan provinces, we would not be able to stop him from compromising us with France and Europe; we could no longer resist him. Hence it follows that it is of the very greatest interest to

us and the Emperor that, if the Bourbons have to fall, it
125 should not be by Garibaldi's agency.

> Cavour to Nigra, 12 July 1860, in D. Mack Smith, *The
> Making of Italy, 1796–1866* (London, 1988) pp. 325–6.

Questions

a Who was the *Galantuomo* in extract (a)? What are the
   alternatives which the Prince sees to the Bourbon
   regime?

b Explain the Prince's reassurance that 'they're sure of him'.

c What were the Garibaldini tactics at Calatafimi; were
   they adopted perforce? Which King was being hailed
   (line 52)?

d Why might Garibaldi's decree (extract c) have worried
   Cavour?

e In what different ways were the Sicilians in extracts (d)
   and (e) dissatisfied with Garibaldi? In extract (e) explain
   'demand a prince for Palermo' (line 91).

★ f Cavour said La Farina had been expelled 'without the
   slightest reason'. Do any of these documents suggest one?
   Why had Cavour sent him to Sicily?

g In extract (f) explain 'compromising us' (lines 121–2).

h Why should the Emperor of France be so concerned at
   Garibaldi's actions?

★ i Did Cavour accurately define Garibaldi's intentions in
   extract (f)?

---

4   Cavour seeks alternatives

(a) *Rapprochement with the Bourbons*

I cannot reject out of hand the offer of an agreement [with
Bourbon Naples] if it is presented to us under French auspices
and with their advice. I agree with you that we are heading
toward a European war, and that is why I cannot break with
5 the Emperor, for we could not wage a European war alone.
Even were we to be helped by England, we could not fight
simultaneously on the two fronts of the Mincio and the Alps.
To reach our goal we must therefore restrain our indignation
and use a certain amount of artifice.
10 What I have done is as follows. When the Naples government
made its first overtures for an alliance I answered that I could not
hear of any such proposal until their government had allowed
Sicilians to dispose of their own destiny. Now if Naples agrees,
the home-rule party there (who want to keep southern auton-
15 omy) will abandon a government that out of cowardice sacrifices

the finest part of their Kingdom. If she refuses, then there will be a clean and open break between Naples and ourselves.

Cavour to Ricasoli, 8 July 1860, in D. Mack Smith, *The Making of Italy, 1796–1866* (London, 1988) p. 316.

(b) *The fear of international repercussion*

20 If Ricasoli reaches the point of saying that we should send France packing and do without French help, I am ready to agree provided we could be certain of the support of public opinion in Europe. For instance, if France opposes our annexing Sicily, I think we could act without her because European public opinion would be on our side. But if France should break with us because we had brought about revolution in 25 Naples, that would be unfortunate, because Europe would think us in the wrong ...

Whoever wins at Naples [ourselves or Garibaldi], it is very important that there should be no aggression against the Roman States.

Cavour to Prince Carignano, the king's representative in Florence, 20 July 1860, in D. Mack Smith, *The Making of Italy, 1796–1866* (London, 1988) p. 317.

(c) *A coup against the Bourbons*

30 If Garibaldi proceeds to the mainland of southern Italy and captures Naples just as he has already taken Sicily and Palermo, he will become absolute master of the situation. King Victor Emmanuel would lose almost all his prestige in the eyes of the Italians, who would look on him as little more than the friend 35 of Garibaldi; and though probably he would remain king, he would merely bask in such reflected glory as this heroic adventurer might decide to allow him.

Garibaldi, if he should reach Naples, would not proclaim a republic, but he would remain dictator, and would refuse to 40 annex southern Italy to Piedmont. His prestige would then be irresistible... . We would be forced to go along with his plans and help him fight Austria. I am therefore convinced that the king must not receive the crown of Italy from Garibaldi's hands, for his title to it would then be precarious, and as a 45 result we would be forced to take arms and try to win greater prestige in Lombardy than Garibaldi has won in Sicily. Only the capture of Verona and Venice would make people forget Palermo and Milazzo.

I have no illusions about the grave and dangerous decision I 50 am advocating, but I believe it is essential if we are to save the monarchic principle. Better than a king of Piedmont should perish in war against Austria than be swamped by the revolution.

The dynasty might recover from a defeat in battle, but if dragged through the revolutionary gutter its fate would be finally sealed.

55 Although I have made up my mind how to act if Garibaldi reaches Naples, it is nevertheless my first duty to the king and Italy to do everything possible to prevent his success there. My only hope of foiling him is if I can overthrow the Bourbon regime before Garibaldi crosses to the mainland – or at least
60 before he has had time to reach Naples. If the regime falls, I would then take over the government of Naples in the name of order and humanity, and so snatch out of Garibaldi's hands the supreme direction of the Italian movement. This will need courage, audacity if you like; it will bring outraged protests
65 from other countries, and may even force us sooner or later to fight against Austria. But it will save us from revolution.

A shipload of arms is therefore being sent to Naples ... [once the coup succeeds] Victor Emmanuel will then accept a Protectorate, and troops will be landed to maintain order and
70 stop Garibaldi's further advance.

Cavour to Nigra, 1 August 1860, in D. Mack Smith (ed.), *Garibaldi* (Florence, 1982) p. 30.

Questions

★ a Why did Cavour think there might be a European war? Who would be the likely combatants? What would be the position of the respective great powers – France, England, Austria and Russia?

b In extract (a) does Cavour sound sincere about the projected alliance with Naples? What was he hoping from it?

c Explain the last sentence in extract (b).

d What justification do these documents show that in the opinion of some contemporaries Cavour was in Napoleon III's pocket?

e How can Cavour's policies in extracts (a) and (c) be reconciled?

f Why did Cavour fear that Piedmont would be forced to help Garibaldi fight Austria?

g How can Cavour claim that a Piedmontese-led overthrow of the Bourbon regime would 'save us from revolution' (line 66)?

h In extract (c) define 'protectorate' (line 69).

★ i In extract (c) if Garibaldi was not a republican (as Cavour admitted) why was he opposed to the immediate annexation of captured Bourbon territory to Piedmont (line 40)?

5 Victor Emmanuel pursues his own policies

(a) *Disposes of Garibaldi*

It was the month of June 1860; Garibaldi had just landed in
Sicily, and the result of his venturesome expedition was not yet
known in Turin, when the French Minister, Baron de Talleyrand,
was ordered to present a note to the Turin cabinet in which the
5 Emperor's government, while bitterly complaining of the fresh
violation of the Law of Nations, referred to the fact that they
were fully aware of the understanding between the Sardinian
cabinet and Garibaldi. After a frank discussion with the Comte
de Cavour, M. de Talleyrand asked to see the King. After his
10 audience with the sovereign, the French minister felt convinced
that His Majesty was far less pleased with the hero's attempt than
people imagined. '*Mon Dieu*', said the monarch to M. de
Talleyrand, 'of course it would be a great misfortune, but if the
Neapolitan cruisers were to capture and hang my poor Garibaldi,
15 he would have brought this sad fate upon himself. It would sim-
plify things a good deal. What a fine monument we should get
erected to him!'

> Memoirs of H. d'Ideville [secretary of the French
> embassy at Turin] in D. Mack Smith, *The Making of
> Italy, 1790–1866* (London, 1988) pp. 333–4.

(b) *Forbids Garibaldi to cross*

You know that when you departed for Sicily your expedition
had not my approval. I have now decided, in the grave condi-
20 tions that exist at this moment, to offer you a suggestion,
knowing the sincerity of your feelings in my regard.

To put an end to the war between Italians and Italians I
counsel you to renounce the idea of crossing to the mainland
with your brave army, provided that the King of Naples
25 pledges himself to evacuate the island and leave the Sicilians
freed to decide their own future. In the event of the King of
Naples not wishing to accept this condition I reserve my full
liberty of action.

General, think over my advice and you will see that it is
30 useful to Italy, towards which you can increase your debt by
showing to Europe that, as you know how to conquer, so you
know how to make the best use of your victories.

> Victor Emmanuel to Garibaldi, 23 July 1860, in A. J. Whyte,
> *The Political Life and Letters of Cavour* (Oxford, 1930) p. 413.

(c) *Endorses Garibaldi's actions*

Garibaldi in Naples. Will regulate himself according to opportunity, either occupying Umbria and the Marches with his

35　troops, or allowing bands of volunteers to go. As soon as
　　Garibaldi is in Naples he will proclaim its union to the rest of
　　Italy as in Sicily. Prevent disorders which would harm our
　　cause. Keep the Neapolitan army in being, for Austria will
　　soon declare war. Let the King of Naples escape, and if he is
40　taken by the people, save him and let him escape.

> Dictated by Victor Emmanuel to his aide, Count
> Trecchi, to be conveyed to Garibaldi, 5 August 1860,
> from G. M. Trevelyan, *Garibaldi and the Making of Italy*
> (London, 1924) pp. 124–5n.

Questions

a　What was the nature of the French complaint; and how
　　did the King attempt to extricate himself?

b　Account for the different treatment of Garibaldi in these
　　three extracts, and extract (b) in section 1.

c　Weigh the sincerity of Victor Emmanuel's comments in
　　extract (a). In what way was his audience important?

d　The Umbria and the Marches belonged to which ruler?
　　What recommendation in extract (c) would have appalled
　　Cavour? Why did Victor Emmanuel want the King of
　　Naples to escape?

VIII   The Final Stage

Introduction

On 11 September 1860 Piedmontese troops invaded the Papal States. They took Ancona, defeated a make-shift papal force at Castelfidardo and, carefully bypassing the region around Rome (the Patrimony of St Peter), advanced to the Kingdom of Naples, now in its death throes against Garibaldi. By this stroke Cavour recaptured the initiative in the *Risorgimento*. Garibaldi was called to order – though he had never ceased a sincere loyalty to Victor Emmanuel – the southern revolution tamed and Piedmontese control imposed throughout Italy.

While a brilliant move, the invasion carried with it a number of risks. The fate of those who had attacked the temporal power of the Pope in 1849 was well known. The changing position and attitude of the great powers, particularly the French, was a constant preoccupation for Cavour. The extent of collusion between himself and Napoleon III, who often acted independently from his foreign ministry, is difficult to determine. Cavour's own achievement lay in the impression he gave of being all things to all men.

Once the Bourbons had been defeated and Italy, in effect, united, the question turned to the form of this new entity. Familiar tensions emerged between unitarians and federalists, radicals and conservatives. Would the new Italy be an expanded Piedmont with Piedmontese institutions? Or an original construct, respecting local traditions and customs? Clearly there were some who were destined to be disappointed.

1   Piedmontese intervention

(a) *Problems with the French*

Yesterday, as you had warned me, I received from Baron de Talleyrand [French ambassador at Turin] the note which threatened to break off relations with us if we continue with our plan to invade the Marches and Umbria. I am deeply sorry about this
5   French move, but I could not compromise the King's dignity by asking him to back out of a project which had already begun.

M. de Talleyand's step did not come unexpectedly. France obviously must not give the appearance of complicity with us in this expedition and she has to make our plan seems an impetuous gesture in the eyes of those who do not fully understand our difficult position. But I am sure we are taking the only step which will allow us to emerge with honour.

You realise all I have done to forestall Garibaldi in Naples. I have been as bold as I possibly could without risking civil war, and I would not have even held back from civil war if I could have hoped that public opinion would support me. But Garibaldi, after conquering Sicily, triumphantly reached Salerno without meeting opposition; it thus became impossible for us to seize Naples by force and steal from him the fruit of victory. The whole of Europe, peoples as well as governments, would have criticised such a mean and thankless act, and the only advantage would have been reaped by Mazzini and his adherents.

That being so, I tried conciliation. By means of a naval captain who is a childhood friend of Garibaldi's, I sent him a letter and tried to persuade him to work together with me. This was only half successful, as Garibaldi went on talking about going to Rome, seizing Venice, taking Nice back, etc. So I had to bring forward my long-mediated plan which Farini had explained to the Emperor at Chambéry.

The day after Farini and Cialdini got back to Turin, I wrote to tell you that the Emperor had unreservedly approved our plan. ... We had every reason to think, therefore, that if we declared immediately that we would stop short of the patrimony of St Peter, and also showed that we had no intention of attacking Austria, we would not receive the Emperor's disapprobation, even though he might scold us in public. ...

I note with gratitude that the Emperor is increasing his garrison in Rome. By reassuring the Catholic world over this so-called danger to the Holy Father, France is doing us a big service. Moreover it will strengthen our position as regards Garibaldi, who I hope will now listen to reason. Once we have avoided being involved by his imprudence in a struggle simultaneously against France and Austria, we will proceed energetically against the party of hot-heads, and so try to regain the confidence of Europe.

Cavour to Nigra, 12 September 1860, in D. Mack Smith, *The Making of Italy, 1796–1866* (London, 1988) pp. 324–5.

(b) *Papal hopes of assistance*

16 September 1860 It is a matter of painful surprise to [Pius IX] that Austria has not yet come to the rescue of the Holy See. ...

22 September At present the Pope's excitement was caused by the slowness of the movements of the French Army. He had been led to expect by Monsieur de Gramont [French ambassador in Rome] that the Emperor Napoleon was going to war with the King of Sardinia for the purpose of driving the Piedmontese troops out of the Holy See and he was now beginning to fear for many reasons that the Emperor would not fulfil his promise. ... The Duke [de Gramont], who deplores these events most sincerely, seems to expect that the Emperor on learning the state of affairs in Rome will take immediate steps to restore the Marches and Umbria to His Holiness ...

25 September Gramont's position is painfully awkward! His colleagues here fancy that his extreme desire to interfere in Italy and crush Piedmont and the whole Italian movement made him believe what he *hoped* and *promised* the Pope in the name of the Emperor, namely that an army of from 50 to 100,000 men would be sent into the heart of Italy to derive Piedmont out of the Papal States and as I have since learnt he added that the stipulation of Villafranca would then be carried out by the combined armies of France and Austria. No wonder that after all these fine promises the Pope should be in a towering passion. ...

2 October It is a matter of general surprise that the French Ambassador has not preferred to resign his post. ...

> Letters from Odo Russell to Lord John Russell, in N. Blakiston (ed.), *The Roman Question* (London, 1962) pp. 126–7, 129–30, 132.

(c) *Cavour defends his actions at home*

How should we have reacted to recent events at Naples? Clearly the Neapolitan government was unable to withstand a handful of volunteers and so lacked the essential conditions for political existence. No restoration of the Bourbons would be possible without foreign help; and that, gentlemen, would have been the greatest possible disaster for Italy. As such a restoration was impossible, and as the Bourbon government had recognised its own powerlessness by surrendering the town of Naples without a fight, morally it was dead. What were we to do? Should we have left that noble part of Italy helpless before events? Should we have allowed the germs of revolution which we had destroyed in northern Italy to multiply elsewhere? No, we could not.

By resolutely seizing the direction of political events in southern Italy, the King and his government prevented our wonderful Italian movement from degenerating; they prevented the factions which did us so much harm in 1848 from exploiting the emergency conditions in Naples after its conquest by Garibaldi. We intervened not to impose a pre-conceived political system on southern Italy, but to allow people there to decide freely on their fate. This, gentlemen, was to be not revolutionary but essentially conservative.

> Cavour to the Piedmontese Senate, 16 October 1860, in D. Mack Smith, *The Making of Italy, 1796–1866* (London, 1988) p. 326.

(d) *From* Punch*, 27 October 1860*

THE RUB.

a Why was Cavour unsurprised at the strength of French protests?

b In extract (a) explain 'the only advantage would have been reaped by Mazzini' (lines 21–2).

c Why did Cavour claim that France was 'doing us a big service' by increasing the Roman garrison? How did this 'strengthen our position as regards Garibaldi' (line 40)?

★ *d* What truth is there for saying that Cavour achieved success by threatening Napoleon with Garibaldi and Garibaldi with Napoleon?

e Account for the different expectations of Napoleon by Cavour and the Pope respectively. When had the Pope been given aid by Austria and France before?

f What needed to be done to fulfil the terms of Villafranca?

★ *g* What was France's eventual response to the Piedmontese invasion of the Papal States?

h Explain Russell's *2 October* entry.

i Explain Cavour's references to 'the germs of revolution' and 'the factions which did us so much harm in 1848' (lines 83, 89).

j How can these documents be used to support the view that Cavour persuaded people to back a revolution on the excuse that this was the way to prevent a revolution?

k What do these documents reveal about Cavour's attitude to Garibaldi's conquest of the south?

l Identify the four men in extract (d); explain their respective remarks.

2   The ways and means of union

(a) *Garibaldi's views on annexation*

'Go back to Sicily with full powers as before, but with one limitation, that of not speaking further of annexation.' [The order] went on to say that annexation would follow as soon as Rome fell, when Garibaldi would offer a kingdom to
5 Victor Emmanuel on two conditions: first, that the officers of the revolutionary army should be compensated for their loss of livelihood and be allowed to transfer their commis-

sions to the regular army; and secondly, 'that His Majesty will promise me on his word as our *Re Galantuomo* to prose-
10 cute the Italian movement until we possess our natural fron-
tiers entire, and that meanwhile he will allow me to march with my army of volunteers to the present boundaries of the state in order to prepare for this final war of liberation.'

> Draft edict by Garibaldi to his representative in Sicily, 14 September 1860, in D. Mack Smith, *Cavour and Garibaldi 1860* (Cambridge, 1985 edn) p. 201.

(b) *Arguments in favour of an assembly first*

A people cannot be said to have full freedom in voting unless
15 there has been previously the free exercise of the right to formulate the alternatives to be voted on. And the exercise of this right cannot be conceived or assured except by means of an assembly freely chosen by the people. ... All the more is this true of Sicily, where the principle of constitutional
20 representation has formed for so long such a vital part of our laws and customs.

> Sicilian petitions to Garibaldi's representative, 3 and 5 October 1860, in D. Mack Smith, *Cavour and Garibaldi, 1860* (Cambridge, 1985 edn) p. 295.

(c) *Against an assembly*

For us in Sicily, annexation means order and justice ... we shall lose none of our rights in doing so, because we shall be joining not Piedmont but Italy. ...
25 To insist on conditions would now imply that we did not want Italian unity: it would signify a wish to separate off from the kingdom of Victor Emmanuel, either to fall again under Francesco, or to turn republican, or else to remain in our present transitory state of uncertainty. ...
30 There are some people who would like five hundred Sicilian deputies to spend time in vain chatter and demand conditions from an executive authority which has no right to grant them. ...

In any case we may be sure that regional liberty cannot be
35 denied us. Parliament will have to provide for it, for in the national parliament all Italy will be represented, and we shall be in a majority by reason of our community of interest with our brothers on the continent. Moreover, let it not be said that we cannot rely on the word of Victor Emmanuel.

> Sicilian Press comment, 12 and 16 October 1860, in D. Mack Smith, *Cavour and Garibaldi, 1860* (Cambridge, 1985 edn) pp. 284–5, 344.

3   The plebiscite

(a) *Wording*

5   I declared that the Southern provinces, owing to the special
conditions under which their revolution had taken place and in
consideration of the importance of their position as regards the
rest of Italy, could not accept the formula that had been
adopted when the people of Tuscany and Emilia had cast their
10   vote. Our country must not *give* herself to another, must not
annex herself, which verb savours overmuch of servitude, but
must rather express her desire that union be achieved. ...
Pallavincino, who is susceptible to great and noble ideals, lis-
tened attentively, and finally burst out with 'Very well, then we
15   will vote for Italy, One and Indivisible, with Victor Emmanuel
for her King. That is, moreover, in perfect harmony with the
Marsala programme.'

> Crispi at a meeting of the provisional government in
> Naples, 8 October 1860, in T. Palamenghi-Crispi (ed.),
> *The Memoirs of Francesco Crispi* (London, 1912) 1,
> pp. 443–4.

(b) *Observing the plebiscite*

October 22 I wanted to see the plebiscite, so I went to St
Francis' square. Opposite the palace the vote was taking place
20   in the church portico. The National Guard was on duty in the
square. Astonishingly, there was perfect order. ...

Yesterday's promise that the vote would be free was honoured,
nevertheless the method of voting left much to be desired. The
ballot box was between two baskets, one full of *yes* slips, the other
25   full of *no* slips. An elector had to choose in clear view of the
Guards and the crowd. A negative vote was difficult or even dan-

gerous to give. In the Monte Calvario district, a man who voted *no* with some bravado was punished with a stiletto blow – assassin and victims are now at the police station.

From the journal of a Swiss writer, in D. Mack Smith, *The Making of Italy, 1796–1866* (London, 1988) p. 321.

(c) *Voting in the Papal States*

30 Your Lordship has probably known the result of the vote for annexation in the Marches and Umbria long before it was whispered from ear to ear in Rome. I have spoken to four English tourists who have passed through Rome after travelling through those provinces, and they report that the enthu-
35 siasm for Unity and Victor Emmanuel has perhaps been even greater than in any other portion of Italy. Even the peasants led by their parish priests, on whose fidelity the Vatican placed almost implicit reliance voted against the temporal rule of the Popes.

Odo Russell to Lord John Russell, 11 November 1860, in N. Blakiston (ed.), *The Roman Question* (London, 1962) p. 137.

(d) *Irregularities*

40 'And you, Don Ciccio, how did you vote on the twenty-first? The poor man started. … The prince mistook for alarm what was really only surprise, and felt irritated. 'Well, what are you afraid of? There's no one here but us, the wind and the dogs.'
… But Don Ciccio had now recovered; his peasant astute-
45 ness had suggested the right reply – nothing at all. 'Excuse me, Excellency, but there's no point in your question. You know that everyone in Donnafugata voted "yes".'
Don Fabrizio [the Prince] did know this; and that was why this reply merely changed a small enigma into an
50 enigma of history. Before the voting many had come to him for advice; all of them had been exhorted, sincerely, to vote 'yes'. … [But the Prince] had, in fact, the disagreeable but distinct impression that about fifteen of them would vote 'no', a tiny minority certainly, but noticeable in the small
55 electorate of Donnafugata. … The cool air had dispersed Don Ciccio's somnolence, the massive grandeur of the Prince dispelled his fears; all that remained afloat now on the surface of his conscience was resentment, useless of course but not ignoble. He stood up, spoke in dialect and gesticu-
60 lated, a pathetic puppet who in some absurd way was right.
'I, Excellency, voted "no", a hundred times "no". I know what you told me: necessity, unity, expediency. You may be right; I know nothing about politics. Such things I leave to others. But

Ciccio Tumeo is honest ... and I don't forget favours done to
65 me! Those swine in the Town Hall just swallowed up my
opinion, chewed it and then spat it out transformed as they
wanted. I said black and they made me say white! ... '

At this point calm descended on Don Fabrizio, who had
finally solved the enigma; now he knew who had been killed
70 at Donnafugata, at a hundred other places, in the course of
that night of dirty wind: a new-born babe; good faith, just
the very child who should have been cared for most, whose
strengthening would have justified all the silly vandalisms.
Don Ciccio's negative vote, fifty similar votes at
75 Donnafugata, a hundred thousand 'no's' in the whole
Kingdom, would have had no effect on the result, which
made it, in fact, if anything more significant; and this
maiming of souls would have been avoided.

From the novel by G. Tomasi di Lampedusa, *The
Leopard* (1988 edn) pp. 92–3, 97–8.

Questions

 a In extract (a) explain 'the Marsala programme' (line 17).
★ *b* In what way was the southern plebiscite assumed to be
    different from the central Italian plebiscites to join
    Piedmont?
★ *c* Why did the wording of the plebiscite probably please
    the radicals more than conservatives; and yet why did
    those seeking southern autonomy or republican status
    find the plebiscite unsatisfactory?
 d Whom did the Vatican rely on to sway the vote?
 e In extract (d) explain 'if anything more significant'
    (line 77).
 f What is the implication of extracts (b) and (d)? Do they
    necessarily contradict extract (c)?

---

4   The conclusion

(a) *Cavour on the need for uniformity*

In my opinion the only way to emerge from this business lies
in using greater firmness. Once we have captured Gaeta we
must make it quite clear that discussion will stop. There must
be no compromise with the various parties, whether these be
5 followers of Mazzini or the Bourbons, revolutionaries or
autonomists. We must then act in accordance with our views
and at once start unifying the various administrative systems.

... Furthermore we need to publish our Piedmontese penal code at Naples, to reform the system of law courts and do a lot
10 else to show we mean to impose a unified system. ... If we show unbending will, people will settle down and adapt themselves to the new regime, because our institutions are in all respects preferable to those from which they were liberated. ... We must impose national unification on the weakest and most
15 corrupt part of Italy. As for the means, there is little doubt: moral force, and, if that is insufficient, then physical force.

> Cavour to Victor Emmanuel, 14 December 1861, in D. Mack Smith, *The Making of Italy, 1796–1866* (London, 1988) pp. 331–2.

(b) *The King's title*

The Chamber of Deputies will tomorrow be voting the law about the title of King of Italy. Some of the Tuscan deputies want Victor Emmanuel II to become Victor Emmanuel I. But
20 I am energetically opposing this, for it is based on sophistical claims which impugn the honour of the dynasty and threaten our principles of public law.

> Cavour to O. Vimercati, 13 March 1861, in D. Mack Smith, *The Making of Italy, 1796–1866* (London, 1988) p. 340.

Questions

★ *a* What was happening at Gaeta?

★ *b* Why was Cavour in such a hurry to introduce reforms – apart from the reasons given in extract (a)?

c What was the significance of the King's title?

d What do these documents reveal about Cavour's attitude to unification?